SKY OF BOMBS, SKY OF STARS

A Vietnamese War Orphan Finds Home

SKY OF BOMBS, SKY OF STARS

A Vietnamese War Orphan Finds Home

Marsha Forchuk Skrypuch

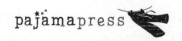
pajamapress

www.pajamapress.ca   info@pajamapress.ca

 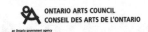

The publisher gratefully acknowledges the support of the Canada Council for the Arts and the Ontario Arts Council for its publishing program. We acknowledge the financial support of the Government of Canada through the Canada Book Fund (CBF) for our publishing activities.

Library and Archives Canada Cataloguing in Publication
Title: Sky of bombs, sky of stars : a Vietnamese war orphan finds home / Marsha Forchuk Skrypuch.
Names: Skrypuch, Marsha Forchuk, author. | Container of (work): Skrypuch, Marsha Forchuk. Last airlift. | Container of (work): Skrypuch, Marsha Forchuk. One step at a time.
Description: Omnibus edition. | Includes bibliographical references and index.
Identifiers: Canadiana 20200163345 | ISBN 9781772780949 (softcover)Subjects: LCSH: Son, Thi Anh Tuyet—Juvenile literature. | LCSH: Children with disabilities—
Biography—Juvenile literature. | LCSH: Adopted children—Canada—Biography—Juvenile literature. |
LCSH: Vietnam War, 1961-1975—Children—Biography—Juvenile literature. | LCSH: Children with disabilities—Hospital care—Canada—Juvenile literature. | LCGFT: Biographies.
Classification: LCC DS559.8.C53 S573 2020 | DDC j959.704/3086914092—dc23

Publisher Cataloging-in-Publication Data (U.S.)

Names: Skrypuch, Marsha Forchuk, author.
Title: Sky of Bombs, Sky of Stars : A Vietnamese War Orphan Finds Home / Marsha Forchuk Skrypuch.
    Description: Toronto, Ontario Canada : Pajama Press, 2020. | Combines previously published Last Airlift, 2011 and One Step at a Time, 2012. | Summary: "Last Airlift is the true story of the last Canadian airlift rescue operation that left Saigon and arrived in Toronto on April 13th, 1975. Son Thi Anh Tuyet was one of the 57 babies and children on that flight. One Step at a Time tells of her adoption into a Canadian family and the challenges she must face."— Provided by publisher.
    Identifiers: ISBN 978-1-77278-094-9 (softcover)
    Subjects: LCSH: Son, Thi Anh Tuyet. | Vietnam War, 1961-1975—Children -- Biography. | Orphans –
Vietnam – Biography – Juvenile literature. | Children with disabilities – Medical care -- Juvenile literature. |
Adopted children – Juvenile literature. | BISAC: JUVENILE NONFICTION / Biography & Autobiography
/ Cultural, Ethnic & Regional. | JUVENILE NONFICTION / Family / Adoption.
    Classification: LCC DS559.8.C53S579 |DDC 959.70430922 – dc23

Cover design—Rebecca Bender
Text Design—Lorena Gonzalez Guillen

Manufactured by Friesens
Printed in Canada
Printed on 45lb Norbrite Cream paper

Pajama Press Inc.
469 Richmond St. E Toronto, ON M5A 1R1

Distributed in Canada by UTP Distribution
5201 Dufferin Street Toronto, Ontario Canada, M3H 5T8

Distributed in the U.S. by Ingram Publisher Services
1 Ingram Blvd. La Vergne, TN 37086, USA

Table of Contents

Historical Note

LAST AiRLiFT:

A Vietnamese Orphan's Rescue from War

With admiration,
to Dorothy Morris
and the late John Morris

VIỆT-NAM CỘNG-HÒA

HỘ-TỊCH

TRÍCH-LỤC BỘ KHAI SANH

Năm một ngàn chín trăm sáu mươi sáu (1966)

Tên, họ đứa nhỏ	NGÔ-THỊ ÁNH-TUYẾT
Phái	Nữ
Ngày sanh	mồ tháng tam năm một ngàn chín trăm sáu mươi sáu - 11giờ36
Nơi sanh	Saigon, 294 Công-Lý
Tên, họ người Cha	///
Tuổi	///
Nghề-nghiệp	///
Nơi cư-ngụ	///
Tên, họ người mẹ	NGÔ-THỊ-HÊ
Tuổi	Hai mươi chín
Nghề-nghiệp	Nội trợ
Nơi cư-ngụ	Saigon, 68 Yên-Đổ
Vợ chánh hay thứ	///

MIỄN LỆ-PHÍ
HỒ-SƠ HÀNH-CHÁNH

Saigon, ngày 14 tháng 5 năm 1966

TRÍCH-LỤC Y BỒN CHÁNH :

Saigon, ngày 23 tháng 9 năm 1977
QUẬN TRƯỞNG QUẬN NHÌ

TRƯƠNG HỮU XƯỚNG

Tuyet's birth certificate

Chapter One
Early April 1975

Tuyet could not remember a time before the orphanage.

She thought that all children lived together in a building with sleeping rooms, a play area, school, and chapel. She remembered sleeping together with the older girls on a wood-slat floor, without blankets or pillows. She would wake up each morning with marks from the wood slats on her cheek.

Tuyet would clean her teeth using her finger and salt. Day and night she wore a pajama-like cotton top and drawstring pants. The nuns would give each child a newly laundered set of clothing every three days or so.

In the morning, she would line up with the other girls. One of the nuns would rip bread from a giant loaf and give a piece to each child. Her meals consisted of fish, rice, plain water. There weren't enough chopsticks to go around, so they used their hands.

The orphanage included boys and younger children—and lots of babies. At the age of eight, Tuyet was one of the oldest. She was expected to help out with the younger ones without being asked. It was her duty, but she didn't mind.

Tuyet would see the older boys in class, when they played together in the indoor courtyard, and at chapel three times a day. The priest who said Mass was the only man she saw in the building, except for the soldiers.

The children stayed inside at all times; it was not safe outside. Tuyet could not remember ever seeing the sky above her head.

When she heard the *whop-whop-whop* of helicopters, Tuyet would hide. She couldn't remember exactly what it was that she was afraid of, but when she put her fingers to her scalp, she could feel dents. She had a

1-2 *Many helicopters were used in the Vietnam war*

large burn scar on her back and another long scar under her chin. She couldn't remember when the injuries happened, but it must have been before the orphanage.

Tuyet remembered the big door opening and American soldiers coming in with stuffed toys, spinning tops, and hard candy. The other children would crowd around the men, competing for attention and gifts. But Tuyet would hide. She wasn't afraid of the Americans, but she had polio. Her left ankle was so weak that she walked on her heel. In order to move forward, she had to push her left knee with her left hand. She had calluses on her knee, because she pushed it so often. She was afraid that if the soldiers saw her foot and weak leg, they would take her to the hospital. And then the doctors would cut her foot open to try to fix it.

Sometimes she played with the other children—simple games with elastics and chopsticks. The children also made a long skipping rope by joining together many elastics. With her weak foot, there was no way Tuyet would ever be able to join in such a game. She could only sit and watch as the others skipped rope.

Some of the children were mean to Tuyet. One boy would crush lit cigarettes on her leg. But there was another boy who was friendly. They would play together as often as they could.

Before school started, Tuyet and the girls would line up. The boys would line up, too. There were even some children from outside the orphanage who came to their school.

Tuyet would sit at her desk, fascinated by the inkwell and pen. She would draw patterns with the ink on paper. Like the other children, Tuyet also had chalk and a slate. She could draw or write something with the chalk, then make it disappear by rubbing it with her hand or a piece of cloth. She vividly remembered using the Vietnamese alphabet, although she couldn't remember what else she learned. When she did well in her lessons, the teacher would paste a small gold star onto her work.

In another room, Tuyet and the other children would gather around the nun who sat in a chair. They would sit on the floor and memorize Bible verses.

The nuns were not always kind. Once, during naptime, Tuyet's eyes were still open as she played with a lock of her hair. A nun came by and told Tuyet to close her eyes and sleep. Then the nun hit her on the fingers, hard, with a bamboo stick.

The nuns would play the piano and they would sing. Tuyet loved that. She remembered one particular night they called "Christmas Eve." She didn't understand what Christmas was, but the nuns gave each child a bowl of special soup instead of their usual meal. The children were allowed to stay up late. The nuns set up a screen and showed them an American movie. It was in English and the children didn't understand the words. But in one scene, a white man and woman kissed each other, and Tuyet and the others giggled in embarrassment.

Another year on that special night, each child was given an orange.

Today, there isn't much more that Tuyet can remember about the orphanage before her life changed forever. And although she cannot remember where she came from, Tuyet does recall two visitors from outside.

"A woman would come to see me. She would bring a young boy. I would sit on her lap for a while and then they would leave. Maybe that was my mother. Maybe the boy was my brother.

"After a while, they stopped coming."

Chapter Two
When things changed
April 11, 1975

Tuyet didn't know about the world beyond her building. But she could hear the soldiers, helicopters, gunfire, and explosions. She had always lived with those sounds in the background.

On the day her life changed, the doors of the orphanage were opened, but instead of soldiers with candy, the children saw a white Volkswagen van screeching to a halt. A man jumped out. He wasn't a soldier or a priest, and he didn't look Vietnamese. He called out to the nuns in a language Tuyet did not understand. Beyond the van, the streets were full of people running. Many carried suitcases; others carried children.

Some of the people were weeping while others were screaming.

The man helped the nuns rush around, packing diapers, formula, water, and bedding. Everything was placed by the door. Tuyet and the older children stared in confusion as the adults gathered boxes and lined them up at the entrance. The nuns carried the babies from their sleeping area and bundled them in blankets. Then each baby was placed in a box. Some boxes were big enough for two babies.

2-1

North Vietnamese tanks enter Saigon

The man had a handful of plastic straps. He read aloud the name printed on each strap, and then a nun would find the right baby and attach the strap to the baby's wrist.

"Son Thi Anh Tuyet," said the man.

Tuyet looked up in surprise. Why was he calling her name? She wasn't a baby. One of the nuns walked up to her. "Let me have your arm," she said. "You'll be going, too."

Tuyet rubbed the snug plastic wristband as the adults loaded the boxes of babies into the back of the van. Suddenly, the man lifted Tuyet into his arms and carried her to the van. Tuyet looked back over his shoulder at the other children—the girls she had slept with for as long as she could remember, that one special boy who had played with her. They all stood huddled together, round-eyed with fear. Was it better to go or stay behind?

As the man set her down on the floor of the van, Tuyet's special friend rushed forward and thrust a small package into her hand.

The back of the van was hot and stuffy, and it was packed so tightly with the boxes of babies that the corner of one box jabbed painfully into Tuyet's hip. But she sat obediently where she had been put. Her left foot and leg hurt most of the time anyway, and she had learned to suffer in silence.

The man climbed into the driver's seat. Tuyet leaned over to get a view of the passenger seat. A frail newborn had been strapped carefully in place beside him.

The van jerked forward. Tuyet turned to stare out the back window as the van slowly pulled away from the orphanage and into the road thick with people and cars. She waved goodbye to her special friend, the nuns, and the other children. She tried to watch them for as long as she could, but the van rounded a corner and the nuns and children disappeared.

Tuyet looked down at the small package she held in her hand, and opened it. Inside was a rosary—a necklace to use for counting prayers—made with pale coral and crystal beads. It sparkled like the gold stars the nuns would award for good work. Tuyet could feel the tears well up in her eyes. Would she ever see that boy again? She let the cool beads slip through her fingers and, for a moment, she thought of nothing but the boy's face. She would try to remember him always. She slipped the shiny beads back into their package and tucked it deep into the pocket of her pants.

Tuyet was jolted out of her thoughts when the van lurched sideways. She gazed out the window at the tangle of traffic and frantic people. In the distance, flames licked up the sides of buildings and smoke billowed high above. Although the sound of gunfire was everywhere, Tuyet felt safe in the van. But she was hot and her hip was sore. She shifted her position so the box wouldn't jab into her so much.

Some of the babies began to wail. The toddlers squirmed and tried to get out of the boxes, but they were packed in so tightly that there was no place to squirm to. The driver was concentrating on the road; there was no one but Tuyet to help the children and babies. She tried to calm them by singing softly and caressing the tear-streaked cheeks closest to her. But they were as hot as she felt. Probably they were as thirsty as she was, too.

Tuyet looked back out the window and marveled at the variety of people in the street. Most of the

2-2

*South Vietnamese civilians flee as Saigon
falls to North Vietnamese forces*

women in the orphanage had been nuns, with their
starched white habits and clinking beads. The priest
was always in robes and the other men were in their
American uniforms. But here, the Vietnamese men
wore white shirts and dark pants. The women were
in long baggy trousers and pastel-colored tops, and
their lush black hair hung down their backs. Some
wore conical bamboo hats. Wherever they were going,

the way was clogged with others going in the same direction.

It seemed like hours, but finally the driver sighed with relief and said something Tuyet couldn't understand. He pointed out the front window.

In front of them stood tall fences topped with barbed wire. People crowded around, trying to push their way through the gate. The soldiers pushed back with their guns. Many of the people reached for the tall wire. One man threw his suitcase all the way over the fence. He clutched onto the wire and pulled himself up. He was almost at the top when a soldier caught him and dragged him down. All of the people appeared frantic to get to the other side.

The van pulled up to a locked gate. Soldiers held back the crowd and the van inched forward. The driver rolled down his window and showed a piece of paper to one of the soldiers. That soldier pushed through the crowd and unlocked the gate, sliding it back just far enough for the van to drive through. The van swayed as people jumped on top of it. Some pounded on the window, and Tuyet hid her face in her hands. Finally,

2-3   *Hercules C-130 aircraft*

the van was on the other side of the gate. Tuyet looked back to see a soldier pull the fence closed again as another held back the crowd.

Without all the people, it seemed suddenly still. The noise from the outside was gone, making Tuyet more aware of the babies and toddlers in the boxes.

"It's all right," Tuyet said in a cooing voice, hoping to comfort the hot and frightened infants. But she had no idea if it *was* all right.

The van drove across a wide empty space and pulled up in front of a strange winged building with a huge door that yawned wide. Many foreign-looking adults scurried about, some carrying toddlers or boxes of babies, others standing by, hands on hips.

Their uniforms made the American soldiers look alike. But Tuyet had noticed before how different their skin looked. Some were pale pink or almost white; others were brown and black. Few were golden like her. And they were always men.

The foreign adults were mostly female. They had pale skin splotched with pink and pale wispy hair in different hues—yellow, orange, brown, and white. Instead of uniforms, they wore complicated clothing, like flowered skirts and pastel dresses with straps, buckles, and ribbons. But their faces still looked the same to Tuyet.

The back door opened and a whoosh of fresher air enveloped her. A man who wasn't a soldier reached in and grabbed one of the boxes that held two tiny babies. Holding the box with care, he rushed to the ramp that led into the winged building. A woman came forward, and then another, and another. As each wrapped her arms around a box, Tuyet pushed the remaining boxes forward so they would be easier to reach. Soon, all the babies were out of the van and Tuyet was left sitting by herself. She wondered if she had been put in the van just to help with the boxes. Would she be going back to her old home now? Back to her special friend?

Other vans and cars pulled up. Workers ran up to those vans and quickly unloaded the children and babies with efficiency. Some older children hopped out, and Tuyet strained to see them more clearly.

But she recognized no one.

A cloud of orange hair poked into the back of Tuyet's van. A hand fluttered to hold the hair in place briefly. Tuyet stared into startling blue eyes and a pink face damp with sweat.

"It's your turn, now," the woman said in Vietnamese. Tuyet scrambled toward the woman, who held out her arms to carry her. But Tuyet shook her head.

"I will walk," she said.

Chapter Three
The Airplane

"What is that place?" asked Tuyet, pointing at the strange winged building.

"A giant airplane called a Hercules," said the woman in Vietnamese. "It will go up into the sky and take us away from the war. It will take you to safety."

Tuyet was amazed. The strange winged building was an airplane! She knew the sound of airplanes. She had heard their roar almost as often as she'd heard the *whop-whop-whop* of helicopters. But this airplane was bigger than her orphanage. She never imagined that an airplane could be so big.

Tuyet sat with her legs poised over the edge of the van

door. Gingerly, she slid down, the heel of her weak foot landing painfully on the oven-hot tarmac. She hopped beside the woman to show she could move quickly, but her feet felt like they were burning up.

"Let me carry you," said the woman. "The pavement is too hot for bare feet."

When she was lifted up, Tuyet had a view of the entire airport and beyond. The airplane she was being taken to wasn't the only one preparing to leave. She could see two others and lots of activity. Above her, the sky was black with spirals of smoke. Where was the black smoke coming from?

Tuyet scanned the lush green expanse of rice paddies beyond the airport runways. And then she saw it: the crashed remains of an airplane with smoke billowing out of it.

She pointed. "That airplane didn't stay up in the air."

The woman's eyes filled with tears. "Don't worry," she said. "We will be safe."

But how could Tuyet not worry?

The entry to the airplane was like a big angled

ramp the width of a room. Tuyet clung to the woman's shoulders as she was carried in. The woman set her down on the floor in the cargo hold amidst boxes of babies, canvas bags, straps, and crates of formula, food, and medicine.

The woman began to push the boxes of babies close together. In order to make sure the boxes wouldn't slide around, she secured them with a long, sticky strap that looped over several boxes at once.

Tuyet saw that it was time to make herself useful. Without being asked, she copied what the woman was doing and strapped in a second row of screaming and wriggling babies.

Soon more people brought box after box through the wide door. Everyone scurried about, finding places for the babies and taping them in.

The giant door closed and the inside of the airplane quickly became hot and stuffy. Worse than the heat was the smell of dirty diapers. Tuyet was used to heat and babies' diapers, but she had never felt so closed in. Her heart pounded. Sweat trickled down her back,

3-1 *Boxed babies strapped in place and ready for takeoff*

getting her shirt all wet. Her hair stuck to her forehead and neck.

The baby boxes covered the floor area of the cargo hold. On the upper level, a row of seats ran along the sides of the aircraft, close to the windows. A set of metal stairs connected the two levels.

Tuyet reached her hand out and caressed the baby

closest to her, but as she cooed a lullaby into the baby's ear, she heard a huge roaring sound. Her body trembled with terror. Was this airplane about to go up in flames like the one she had seen in the rice paddy?

Tuyet felt a hand on her arm. She looked up. It was one of the women who spoke her language.

"That's just one of the engines," the woman explained. "The pilot turned it on to cool the air. There are three more engines, so don't be frightened when they start up."

Tuyet nodded. Maybe it would be fine.

Just then, a small door at the front of the airplane was pulled open from the outside. Four North Vietnamese soldiers stepped in, armed with machine guns. They looked angry.

The woman appeared frightened, but she stood and walked up to the soldiers. "Everything is in order," she said.

"We need to see their papers," said one of the soldiers, pointing his machine gun at the babies and children.

The woman hurried to the cockpit and came back with a stack of forms. She handed them to one of the soldiers. He examined each form carefully, matching them up with the wrist straps as he did so. A baby not far from Tuyet had no wrist strap.

"You have no papers for her," he said. "And no papers for that one," he added, pointing to an older toddler who was trying to stand up in his box.

The woman's face stayed calm and strong, but her lips were a pale thin line. "Just a minute." She headed back to the cockpit.

For a minute, nothing happened.

Then, suddenly, one of the pilots burst out of the cockpit. He wore a fancy hat with gold braid, and his face was purple with rage. He hollered something in another language at the two soldiers.

The sight of the raging pilot terrified Tuyet, but it also startled the soldiers. They backed out of the door and ran down the steps. The pilot pulled the door shut with all his might and locked it from the inside, sighing with relief. He took off the hat with the fancy braid.

All at once, Tuyet understood. The pilot had tricked the soldiers into thinking he was an important commander who had to be obeyed. It made her smile.

The pilot went back into the cockpit and the woman stepped out again. She looked almost happy.

"You need to get into a seat," said a different woman, who crouched down in front of Tuyet. "Can you walk, or do you want me to carry you?"

Tuyet was afraid that she might lose her balance and hurt the babies if she tried to cross the middle of the cargo hold without help. The babies and extra supplies were so closely packed together. Tuyet reached out her arms and the woman picked her up. She held Tuyet above the babies and helped her to the steps and into a seat by the window, not far from the cockpit.

"I will strap you in," the woman said kindly.

For a moment, Tuyet's heart thumped with panic. She did not want to be tied down. "Can I get out if I need to?"

"Of course you can. Watch." The woman flicked the metal clamp with her finger and the seatbelt popped open. Tuyet tried opening and closing the seatbelt herself a few times. She began to relax.

"But you must be strapped in when the airplane

takes off," the woman added, then she straightened up and walked down the aisle.

At that moment, even though Tuyet was in an airplane jam-packed with babies and children—along with the adults who were working to save them—she felt utterly alone. She remembered the rosary her special friend had given her. Holding it would make her feel better. She reached into her pocket. But her pocket was empty.

The package was gone.

The rosary must have dropped out in the van, or maybe later, when she was helping with the babies. Tears filled her eyes and spilled down her cheeks. She tried to breathe slowly, to make the tears go away. She didn't want anyone to see that she was crying, so she closed her eyes.

Her hands felt something soft. She opened her eyes. A cloth doll. She looked up. One of the women, smiling, hovered over her. Tuyet hugged the doll to her chest.

"Thank you," she said, looking into the woman's gold-colored eyes.

The woman patted Tuyet's hand. "It's going to be fine."

Tuyet had never owned a doll before. The visiting soldiers sometimes brought dolls to a few of the children in the orphanage, but never to Tuyet. She held the doll up to her face and breathed in its fresh newness. For just a few moments, she was able to forget losing her friend, losing the life she had known. Maybe everything would be all right.

Tuyet looked out the window. From where she sat, she had a clear view of the smoking plane in the distance. She closed her eyes and clasped the doll to her chest.

The plane moved forward. Tuyet exhaled in relief. Soon they would be away from here. She didn't know if she was looking forward to the future, but at least the uncertainty would soon be over.

The Hercules shuddered to a stop.

Tuyet opened her eyes and looked out the window. Two people stood on the runway, in front of the airplane! Didn't they realize they might have been run over? How had they got past the soldiers and the fence?

Tuyet squinted to get a better look. The man wore the distinctive collar of a priest. He was holding tight

3-2   *Major Cliff Zacharias*

to the hand of a girl who looked about the same age as Tuyet.

The pilot called out, "You've got to get out of the way!"

"You must take this girl with you!" the priest hollered back.

"We're not allowed to," shouted the pilot.

"Then we'll stand here in front of the plane."

The cockpit door opened. The pilot stomped out,

looking angry and frustrated. He unlatched the door at the front of the airplane and pushed it open. Moments later, the girl's head appeared in the doorway.

Tuyet looked out the window, where the priest now stood alone. He bowed in thanks and walked off the runway.

The pilot led the girl to an empty seat in front of Tuyet and quickly strapped her in. Then he headed back to the cockpit.

The girl wept quietly. Tuyet leaned forward and said, "It will be okay."

The second engine began to roar, then the third and, at last, the fourth.

"Get ready for takeoff," called the pilot through the speaker system.

Tuyet leaned back into the seat and clutched her doll. Under her breath, she whispered, "Please let this plane fly, please let this plane fly."

The Hercules moved again. From where Tuyet sat, she could see one of the giant wings. Suddenly, part of the wing folded down. Oh no! Was this how the other plane had crashed? Tuyet whimpered.

"It's the wing flaps," said the woman in the seat behind her. "They're supposed to do that."

Tuyet closed her eyes and repeated her wish, "Please let this airplane fly!"

Just as the wish left her lips, the Hercules lifted. It angled up to the sky so sharply that Tuyet could feel blood rushing to her head and the skin on her face pulling tight. The babies, who had been whimpering half-heartedly, began to scream. The airplane went higher. Babies cried louder. Tuyet felt like the plane was going straight up into the air. Her ears popped. She was afraid to breathe.

The plane leveled out. The babies stopped screaming and suddenly it was silent. Then the woman behind her said, loud enough for everyone to hear, "We're safe now."

Tuyet felt tears of relief rise in her throat. They were safe!

But she was still afraid.

Chapter Four
Linh

Once the plane was in the air, the adults unbuckled their seatbelts and went down the metal steps to get to the babies. Tuyet opened the buckle to her own seatbelt. It felt good to have it off. She leaned forward to speak to the sobbing girl.

"My name is Tuyet," she said. "I am happy to meet you."

It took the girl a moment to compose herself enough to answer. "My name is Linh*," she said hesitantly. "I am happy to meet you as well, Tuyet."

"We should help with the babies," said Tuyet. "I can smell a lot of dirty diapers."

---

* Not her real name, which has been changed to protect her privacy.

4-1   *Aid workers assist the children during the flight*

That made Linh smile. "Good idea."

Tuyet gingerly got out of her seat and made her way down the steps. Linh was not far behind. When Tuyet looked back, she saw Linh glance at her weak leg.

"Do you need help?" asked Linh.

"I can manage on my own," said Tuyet. She hated it when people assumed she couldn't do things because of her foot.

Once she was in the lower part of the Hercules,

Tuyet crawled on her hands and knees between the crying babies. It was so crowded with boxes and supplies that Tuyet did not want to risk losing her balance. The women didn't have to tell her what to do. She changed diapers when she found them wet, and she gave bottles of water to babies who felt hot.

Linh stood by awkwardly, staring at the organized chaos all around her. She didn't seem to know what to do.

"Take this baby," said Tuyet, reaching into one of the boxes and thrusting a screaming baby into Linh's arms. "She probably has gas. Hold her up to your shoulder and pat her on the back. Walk around. The movement will help."

Linh followed the instructions while Tuyet continued looking after the babies. Some time later, Linh came back, a sleeping baby in her arms. Tuyet gently took the baby from her and set him in his box.

"How do you know what to do with babies?" Linh asked.

Tuyet met her eyes. "I've been looking after babies for as long as I can remember."

Linh continued to take directions from Tuyet and,

between the two of them, they settled many babies. Being busy helped Tuyet relax. And with the company of Linh, Tuyet didn't feel quite so alone.

As they worked, they overheard some of the women speak to each other in a language that they couldn't understand.

"They're speaking English," Linh told Tuyet. "Be careful how you answer when people say things to you in English."

"I don't know any English," said Tuyet. "How could I possibly answer?"

"Whenever someone asks you something in English, answer, *No*," said Linh. "That will stop them from doing what they were going to do."

Tuyet practiced the English word under her breath. It was hard to believe that one simple word could be the answer to everything in English, but she was grateful for Linh's advice.

The great Hercules airplane landed in Hong Kong. Tuyet, Linh, and the others were taken to a hospital.

A man, who was dressed in white with a mask over his face, shone a light into Tuyet's ears.

"Good," he said in Vietnamese.

He listened to her heart and had her breathe in and out. He also examined her weak foot and leg, and that worried Tuyet. But he wrote something on his clipboard, and his eyes crinkled into a smile.

"You are healthy enough."

4-2   *Tuyet and other children insidethe Hercules during the flight. Captain Dessureault of 426 Squadron is in the foreground, holding one of the children.*

Linh was examined next and she got the same good news.

Tuyet, Linh, and the babies and children declared healthy enough to travel were taken to a section of the Hong Kong hospital where they could rest and recover. For the next few days, they were bathed, dressed in clean clothing, and fed lots of good food.

The orphans who were too sick to travel were taken to a different part of the hospital for treatment.

After their few days' rest, Tuyet, Linh, and the other healthy orphans boarded a Canadian Pacific flight. The boxes of babies, care workers, and children took up a good part of the airplane, but there were regular passengers on it, too. Many pitched in to help feed babies, change their diapers, and rock them to sleep.

There were more flights between Hong Kong and Toronto, but they all blended into one long dream. It felt as if time had stopped. Vaguely, Tuyet remembered singing songs with Linh and trying to get babies to laugh. She remembered feeding the older toddlers a rice and broth mixture, and that's what she and Linh also ate. That, and plenty of bananas.

4-3   *Aid workers helping some orphans in Hong Kong*

The airplane landed in Vancouver and they changed planes one last time. This time, it was an Air Canada commercial flight.

A few hours later, they arrived at the Toronto airport.

A care worker pinned on Tuyet's shirt a piece of paper with the number 23 on it. Then the children and babies were taken off the airplane in numerical order.

The first thing Tuyet noticed when she approached the open door was cold air blowing on her face.

Someone quickly draped a white blanket around her shoulders and she clasped it around herself for warmth. It was always hot and humid in Saigon; Tuyet had never felt air like this before. She gulped the breeze into her lungs as if it were a cool, soothing drink.

She sniffed the air, and the scent brought back a distant memory of freshly ploughed earth. No smell of smoke.

No sound of war.

Then Tuyet looked up into the sky, and she gasped. It was like a soft blanket of black, but she could see points of sparkling white light. Had the war followed her here?

She pointed up and asked a care worker who stood by her side, "Are those bombs?"

"No," said the man. "Those are stars. They are beautiful to look at and they will not harm you."

Stars. Tuyet remembered the bits of foil her teacher would stick onto her schoolwork when she did well. Those were called stars, too. She looked back up at the sparkling points of light. Stars were *real?* The sight of so many of them in the sky made her feel proud. It was as if

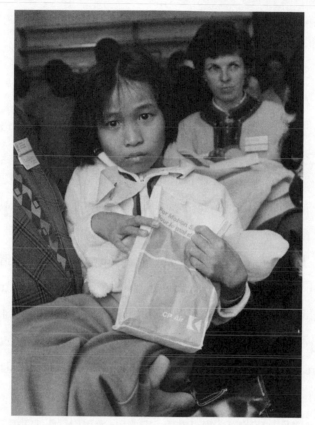

4-4   *Tuyet arrives in Toronto*

the sky was telling her that she had done a good job, helping all those babies through their long journey together.

Tuyet knew that she could walk down the steps
from the airplane on her own. But she was so tired that

she didn't protest when the care worker picked her up and carried her down.

Suddenly, a bright flash startled her.

And another.

Tuyet whimpered in fear. She buried her face in the care worker's neck.

"It's okay," said the man. "Those aren't guns. They are just cameras. These people are taking your picture for the newspapers."

Tuyet knew about flash cameras. Once, a soldier had brought a flash camera to the orphanage. Tuyet had thought it was a new kind of weapon and she had stayed well hidden. Shortly before she was evacuated, a nun had taken her picture. But that camera was small and Tuyet trusted the nun.

Tuyet poked her head up and squinted, trying to get a good view of the cameras in the dark. The care worker was right. The cameras were much bigger than any she had seen before. But they were definitely not weapons.

Once everyone was off the airplane, they were all loaded onto a bus. Tuyet and Linh sat beside each other.

Tuyet said, "What is going to happen to us now?"

"I'm not sure," said Linh, gripping one of Tuyet's hands in her own. "But remember to say no if some-one asks you something in English. It's the only way to stay safe."

Tuyet looked out the window as the bus pulled away from the airport. The crowds of people were still there, flashing away with their cameras. Tuyet didn't want to look at those people. She gazed up into the night sky, willing the stars to calm her and fill her with courage.

The bus jolted forward and Tuyet was reminded of the earlier van ride that had taken her away from everything familiar. Where would this bus take her? Once the rest of the children in the van had all been adopted, would the adults send her back to Saigon? Or would she go to work in an orphanage in this strange city? Would Linh work with her, or would her friend be adopted?

As the bus maneuvered through the quiet streets of nighttime Toronto, Tuyet was struck by how differ-ent the city looked from Saigon. There were no people running through the streets with their suitcases, no soldiers with guns, no fires in the distance, no smoke. Just fresh, cold air and tall buildings that sparkled with multicolored lights. Some of the lights outlined pictures and others spelled out words. Some of the letters were the same as in the Vietnamese alphabet. Tuyet tried to sound the words out, but nothing made sense.

It wasn't long before the bus stopped. A pale brick building loomed out of the darkness.

"Maybe this is where we're going to live now," said Tuyet.

Linh didn't answer. Her eyes were wide with fear. They got off the bus. Linh gripped one of Tuyet's hands in her own, and the two girls slowly walked forward with the rest of the tired group.

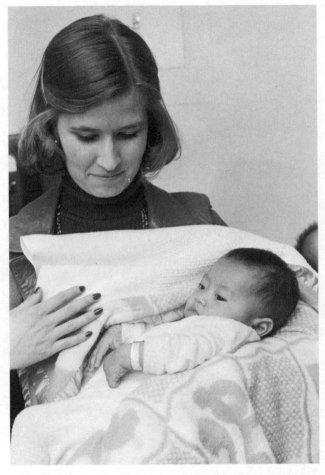

5-1

*A care worker looks after
a baby at Surrey Place*

Chapter Five
Surrey Place

The children were lined up by numbers once again. A man looked at the information on Tuyet's wrist band and wrote something onto a form. Next, someone with a camera took her picture, but this time it didn't flash. Tuyet watched with curiosity as a piece of paper came out of the camera. The man held it up to her and smiled. It was a picture of a sad-looking girl.

"That's you," said Linh.

Tuyet blinked in surprise. She had never seen a picture of herself before, and there were no mirrors in the orphanage. Did she really wear her sadness on her face for all to see?

Tuyet watched the man glue the picture onto the information form.

Next, she was taken to a room with rows of iron beds. Children, some of them crying, occupied the beds. More adults stood by, dressed in white.

A man sat Tuyet on a bed, listened to her chest, and looked inside her mouth with a flashlight and a

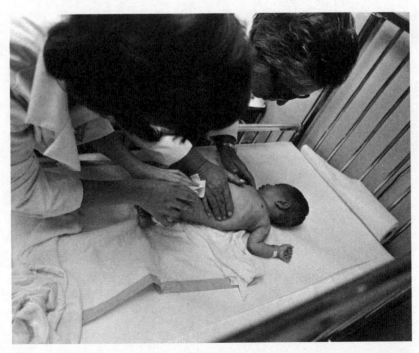

5-2   *Medical staff examine a baby at Surrey Place*

stick. He held her hair up and looked into her ears. Then he used a little hammer to tap her good knee. He looked at her weak knee and foot, but he was so gentle, it didn't hurt at all. He wrote something on her information sheet.

Next, he held her arm firmly and pressed a metal contraption on it. *Bang.* Tuyet jumped.

"All done," said the man in Vietnamese.

Tuyet looked down at the place on her arm where the metal contraption had been, and saw a circle of little pinpricks. It didn't hurt.

A man who was Vietnamese came to the room and took her by the hand. Tuyet had been so focused on what was happening to her that she had lost track of Linh. Now she looked frantically around the room.

"Do you know where Linh is?" she asked the man.

"Probably upstairs," the man answered. "Once you're finished with the medical examination, I'll take you up to join her."

The rest of her examination didn't take long. The man took Tuyet out of the room and into the hallway, where he stopped in front of two metal doors.

"This is an elevator," he said. "Quicker than stairs."

The doors opened and they both stepped inside a small room. The doors closed. Tuyet could feel panic rise in her stomach, but the man was calm and the doors opened quickly again. They stepped out into a big room, where metal beds and bassinettes were arranged in rows.

Linh sat on one bed, and she held a stuffed bear on her lap. "Tuyet!" she called. "Take this bed beside me."

On the bed next to Linh sat a colorful stuffed doll with a plaid skirt and button eyes.

"Is that for me?" asked Tuyet.

"Yes," the man answered and smiled down at her. "Each child gets a toy."

Tuyet reached for the doll. Then she remembered. Where was the doll she'd been given on the flight? It had felt so good to have something of her own. How could she have left it behind? Tuyet hugged the new doll to her chest. This one she would not forget.

Tuyet pulled herself up onto the bed beside Linh. The man brought each girl a glass of juice and a

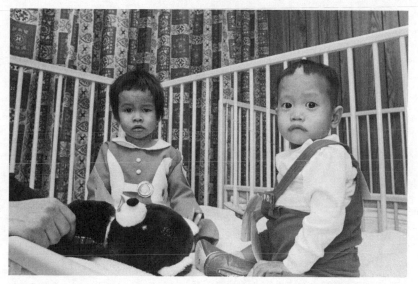

5-3   *Toddler with new bear, Surrey Place*

cookie. As Tuyet sat there, nibbling on the cookie and feeling the warmth of her friend by her side, she felt happy.

"This is not bad," she said with a grin.

"I am pretty sure we won't be staying here," said Linh. "I think we will be given to families."

Tuyet had heard about children getting new families. At the orphanage in Saigon, some of children were taken away. The nuns said they had gone to new families. But none of the children ever came back to tell the others what happened next. Did the new families feed them? Did they make them do chores? Tuyet didn't know. She looked around the room and took a deep breath. It could be worse. This place was clean and bright, and there were no sounds of war.

Tuyet thought about that woman and boy who visited her in the orphanage. Were they her family? She thought of the special boy at the orphanage. Was he her family, too?

She clutched her new doll and thought of the other doll and the rosary she had lost. Were families as replaceable as dolls and rosaries? Linh was now Tuyet's only friend. Tuyet felt tears welling up inside her. Would Linh be lost to her now, as well?

"Will you promise to stay with me always?" Tuyet asked Linh.

"It is not up to us," said Linh. "But I will try."

"If they try to take you away from me, you can just say *no*," said Tuyet.

Linh smiled. "Good idea."

With that, Linh finished the last of her juice and cookie. She curled up on the cot and, hugging her new stuffed bear, closed her eyes.

Tuyet walked over to her own bed and sat down. Linh was already deep in an exhausted slumber. Even Linh did not need Tuyet. She felt so alone.

The women in white carried more babies into the room. Tuyet longed to help. In the airplanes, it had felt so good to prove that she was useful.

The babies looked clean and well fed. But as soon as the women put them into their own bassinettes, the babies began to scream.

Tuyet felt like screaming, too. The babies must be exhausted. Why were they crying?

As she stared at the babies, Tuyet suddenly realized the problem. When the babies were put to bed at the orphanage, they were always close enough to touch. Here, the babies were separated from each other. They weren't used to being alone.

Tuyet stood up. She scanned the room to see if the man who spoke Vietnamese was still there, but he had left. She went up to one of the workers, a woman with yellow hair held in place with a pink elastic band.

Tuyet tapped the woman's arm. "The babies," she said. "They want to be close to each other."

The woman stared back at Tuyet, her face blank. She didn't understand Vietnamese.

Tuyet went up to Linh and shook her shoulder. Linh sat up, rubbing the sleep from her eyes.

"The babies are upset," said Tuyet. "They're too far apart."

Linh gave a huge yawn and stood up. "I guess we'll have to show them."

Tuyet smiled. She knew she could count on Linh to help her.

The two girls pulled blankets off the beds and laid them out in the middle of the floor. Tuyet picked up one of the crying babies. A care worker walked over to take the baby away from her.

Tuyet held up one hand. "*No*," she said.

Linh picked up another baby. They placed the babies on the blanket so close that they were touching. The babies stopped crying. Tuyet and Linh picked up two more babies and placed them on the blanket, so close to the others that they, too, were touching. Those babies stopped crying, as well.

One of the workers smiled in understanding. "Come," she said to the others. "Let's get these babies together so they can get some sleep."

Once the babies and toddlers were asleep, the room seemed unnaturally quiet to Tuyet. All her life, she had been surrounded by noise.

"Can I sleep beside you on your cot?" Tuyet asked Linh.

"I would like that," said Linh.

In no time, the two exhausted girls were fast asleep. In the morning, the workers turned their efforts to Linh and Tuyet. Each had to give up her clothing. They had a shower in a white-tiled bathroom that smelled of antiseptic. After the shower, they came out, shivering, and were wrapped in towels. The workers gave them each a pair of pants, a sweater, socks, and a small white cotton item.

"What is this?" Tuyet asked Linh, holding up the small bit of cotton.

"Underwear," said Linh. "You put it on underneath your pants."

The thought made Tuyet giggle. It seemed so un-necessary. At the orphanage, Tuyet had never worn such a thing, just the pajama-like top and drawstring bottoms. She shrugged and put on the underwear. She guessed she would have to get used to more strange Canadian customs.

Tuyet's pants and sweater fit well enough, but she couldn't get the socks to stretch over her weak foot. Linh got shoes, but none fit Tuyet, so she left her feet bare.

Over the next few days, everything settled into a rou-tine. It reminded Tuyet of the orphanage. There were no lessons or chapel, and no one rapped Tuyet's knuck-les with bamboo, but eating and sleeping and washing and playing were done to a schedule.

Was this what her life would be like from now on? Tuyet didn't mind. She had the babies to help with. She had her friend Linh beside her. No helicopters flew overhead. And there was no war.

But a few days later, just as she was getting used to the routine, everything changed. People came in—men and women who didn't speak Vietnamese. Each couple took a baby away. Would all the babies be taken away? And once they were gone, where would she and Linh go? Would they be sent to another place filled with babies?

Then, one morning, it was Linh's turn.

Tuyet watched in despair as a woman and man with kind smiles sat with Linh and talked to her with hand gestures. Linh grinned with joy. She did not use the word *no*. Linh glanced over at Tuyet and a look of concern clouded her face. She motioned to the man and woman that she would be back. Then she approached Tuyet.

"They want to be my new family," she said.

"You promised you would say no," said Tuyet. "I want you to stay here with me."

"You'll be getting a family, too," said Linh. "*No* won't work." She hugged Tuyet. "I will never forget you."

Tuyet didn't hug Linh back. She pushed her away.

"Have a good life," she said, limping over to hug one of the babies before Linh could see the tears in her eyes.

The Child Welfare Act
ADOPTION ORDER

In the   County   Court of the   County   of   Brant

HIS HONOUR JUDGE

E.O. FANJOY   Thursday   , the   15th

IN CHAMBERS   day of   January   , 19 76.

In the matter of   Thi Anh Tuyet Son

resident in the Province of Ontario and born or alleged to be born in

the   City   of   Saigon

in the   Gia Dinh   of in   in the

Province of South Vietnam   , on the   6th   day

of   August   , 19 66.   , as appears by the

Registration Number   65463   on the certificate of birth

registration issued by South Vietnam

AND IN THE MATTER OF *The Child Welfare Act.*

Upon the Application of   John Charles Morris

of the   City   of   Brantford   in the   County   of

Brant   and   Dorothy Elaine Morris   his wife, both

resident in the Province of Ontario, for an order for the adoption of the said child;

Upon Reading the certificate of the   Local Director   under the said Act
(Director or local director)

and upon considering what was alleged by or on behalf of the said applicants and being satisfied

that compliance has been made with the said Act:

It is Ordered:

1. That   Thi Anh Tuyet Son   be and is hereby adopted as the

child of   John Charles Morris   and   Dorothy Elaine Morris

2. That the name of the child shall be   Tuyet Ruth Morris

Entered O.B. '4'
Date 15/1/76
Initials J.A.W.

20-00-028 (4/73)   (Judge)

Chapter Six
Tuyet's Turn

Tuyet sat at a table alone, clutching the doll she had been given on her first night at Surrey Place.

She pulled off bits from a piece of bread and put them in her mouth. She did not feel hungry. She felt overwhelmingly sad, but Tuyet chewed on the bread anyway. After all, if she no longer had a job to do, they might stop feeding her.

Linh had not been gone for more than an hour, but it felt like forever to Tuyet. The loneliness sat like a weight on her shoulders.

One of the workers said something in English to Tuyet. She looked up.

Standing beside the worker was a woman holding onto the hands of two girls. The older child had a face that looked similar to the woman's and the younger one had a lovely golden complexion. A friendly-looking man stood beside them, grinning. In his arms, he carried a toddler who was surely Vietnamese. Confused, Tuyet looked back at the woman. Her eyes were brimming with tears. The girls looked as if they could barely contain their excitement.

All at once, Tuyet understood. Each couple had chosen only one baby. And Linh was the only child chosen by the last couple. All of them had found families. But this couple already had three children. What they needed was a helper.

And they had chosen Tuyet for the job.

At first, her heart felt crushed with disappointment. Deep down, she had hoped to be treated like the other children, but when had *that* ever happened?

Tuyet pasted on a brave smile, but she was still afraid. Did they know about her weak leg and foot? Maybe they wouldn't even want her as a helper once they saw her foot. All her life, she had worked hard to prove herself useful. She would just have to prove herself once more. Better to get it over with right away.

Tuyet put her bread down and pushed herself into a standing position. With her doll clutched in one hand, she limped to their side of the table and waited, her eyes cast down. She expected them to walk away.

But they didn't.

Tuyet felt a pair of arms around her shoulders. The woman knelt beside her and held her tight. She said something in English, but the only word Tuyet could understand was *Mom*.

Tuyet's memory flashed to the woman who had visited her in the orphanage in Saigon. Had that been her mom—the woman who stopped visiting? Was that woman no longer Tuyet's mom?

Did this woman really want to be her mom? Tuyet was thrilled at the possibility. But what if this woman changed her mind, too? Tuyet became anxious to leave, *now*, before anyone had a chance to reconsider.

The care workers didn't want Tuyet to leave bare-foot. It was cold for April, and it was raining. They found her a pair of white rubber boots that were so huge they reached past her knees. It was hard enough to walk barefoot, but in these boots, it was almost impossible. Mom put Tuyet's doll into her purse and took one of Tuyet's hands. The man held the toddler on his hip with one hand. Then he took Tuyet's other hand, while the two young girls walked beside them.

On their way out of Surrey Place, one of the workers wrote something on a piece of paper and gave it to Mom. Tuyet wondered what the paper said, but once they were outside, she didn't give it another thought.

She lifted her face to the sky. It wasn't black anymore and there were no stars. Now the sky was full of billowy gray clouds, and big droplets of water splashed on her face. It was as if the sky were crying for all that Tuyet had lost. But the cool rain that splattered on her upturned face also felt soothing, as if it could wash away the past. With each step away from the building, Tuyet felt a little less anxious.

The family hadn't changed their mind yet.

The man opened the back door of a car and the two girls climbed in. Mom opened the front passenger

6-2   *The Morris family. From left, Lara, John,*
Tuyet, Beth, Dorothy, Aaron

door and motioned for Tuyet to get in. It wasn't an easy job in the big white boots. So the man lifted her up to the seat, pulled off her boots, and put them into the trunk. He didn't seem to mind the look of her weak foot and leg at all. Tuyet slid over to the middle of the front seat. The man climbed into the driver's seat and Mom sat on her other side, with the toddler on her lap.

She took the doll out of her purse and gave it back to Tuyet, who held it close.

As they drove away, the older girl leaned forward and said to Tuyet, "My name is Beth."

Tuyet turned around to get a better look at the two girls in the back. Both looked so happy and relaxed, like they belonged. Tuyet wondered what it would feel like to belong. She just couldn't imagine it.

"My name is Lara," said the other girl. "I'm adopted, too, but Beth is homemade."

Whatever the girl said must have been funny, because the two adults chuckled.

Beth pointed to the toddler and said, "That is Aaron. He's adopted, too."

Tuyet was pretty sure she understood three things about that conversation: the older girl's name was *Beth*, the younger girl was named *Lara*, and the baby was *Aaron*.

She pointed to herself and said, "Tuyet."

Beth clapped her hands and grinned. "Pleased to meet you, Tuyet."

Lara bounced up and down. "Hello, Tuyet!"

Beth pointed to the man who sat beside Tuyet, and said, "*Cha*."

Cha meant *Dad*.

Tuyet knew about moms. In the orphanage, many of the children would talk longingly of their moms. But a dad was a different matter. Tuyet had listened as some children talked about their dads, but they didn't seem very real. She had never actually seen one. To her, a dad was like a made-up person, a ghost.

She thought back over the last few days. So many babies and children had been chosen by couples—men and women together. She realized that each family had a man and a woman in it. So here, in this country, it seemed, dads were more than ghosts.

Out of the corner of her eye, Tuyet looked at this man, this *actual* dad. He seemed friendly.

Tuyet listened to the girls chattering away in the back. Beth seemed to be around four years old and Lara was a bit younger. Aaron couldn't be more than two.

Tuyet heard the crinkle of paper from the back seat. She turned to look. Beth had opened up a small package of crackers. She gave one to Tuyet and one to Lara. Tuyet looked at the cracker. She was not in the habit of saying no to food. Who knew when she would have a chance to eat again? But she was so nervous that her stomach was doing flip-flops. She wasn't sure she would be able to eat.

Beth popped her own cracker, whole, into her mouth and chewed. Lara took nibbling bites. Tuyet didn't want to say no. Even though Linh had told her that *no* was the magic word in English, she was afraid to use it now. Maybe they would return her to Surrey Place if she didn't like the food they gave her.

She took a bite of the cracker, then another.

Soon it was gone.

Beth handed her a second cracker and she ate that one, too. But then Beth gave her another, and another. Tuyet didn't want any more crackers, but she was afraid to refuse them. She did not want the family to be angry with her.

Tuyet's stomach lurched with queasiness. She wasn't sure if it was from so many crackers, the car ride, or the excitement of being with this family. She looked behind at Beth and was thankful to see that the package of crackers was empty.

Tuyet looked out the front window and watched trees and buildings speed by, but that didn't help her stomach. She could feel the crackers rising in her throat. What should she do? She couldn't very well throw up in this fancy car! She would be taken back to Surrey Place for sure.

Tuyet swallowed and tried to breathe slowly. She put both hands over her mouth. She tried to swallow down a gag.

They traveled in silence for a while, and Tuyet concentrated on not being sick. The car turned off the busy road and onto smaller winding ones. Tuyet looked out the window and saw houses, each one a different color. Some houses were made of wood and others were stone or brick. Flowers and sometimes big trees grew in front of them. Each house sat on a smooth carpet of green—it reminded Tuyet of rice paddies. The sight calmed her. It was good to know that one of her favorite foods grew in Canada.

For a moment, she forgot about her upset stomach.

Dad pulled into the driveway of a gray brick house with cheerful red trim. Flowers grew up through rocks, and a rice paddy sat in front.

"We're home!" cried the girls in the back. As soon as the car stopped, Lara opened her door and hopped out. Beth was close behind.

Now that the car was no longer moving, Tuyet hoped that her stomach would settle down.

Mom opened up the passenger door and got out with Aaron in her arms. Dad opened up his door and went to the trunk to bring Tuyet her boots. He set them on the driveway in front of her.

Just as she was sliding her feet into the boots, Tuyet felt her stomach roiling once again. She put her hands over her face, but this time she couldn't stop. Vomit shot out of her mouth and all over her clothing, doll, and boots. She stumbled forward, anxious to keep the vomit away from the car.

To her horror, the last of the vomit came out over Dad's shoes.

Chapter Seven
Home

Viet orphan joins city family

By MARY-ANNE HLADISH
Expositor Staff Writer

th2 Morrises already have two
adopted children of mixed racial
origin.

the Sunday get-together it was
amazing to observe how all the
children communicated with

wait until September to give
Tuyet time to learn English.

Mr. Morris said Tuyet has had

7-1   *Headline from the Brantford Expositor, April 23, 1975*

Tuyet was afraid. She held her breath. What would this man do to her now?

Would he return her to Surrey Place?

His voice didn't sound angry. She couldn't understand the words, but she could tell he was not upset. Tuyet looked up. He was smiling. She had just ruined his shoes and he was smiling! He didn't seem to mind at all.

Lara tugged on Tuyet's hand and grinned. "Don't worry," she said. "I throw up sometimes, too."

"Come on," Beth said excitedly. "I want to show you around."

"She needs a bath first," said Mom.

Tuyet looked at all the moving lips and tried to understand. It was impossible to know what the words meant, but Tuyet could tell that nobody was angry with her.

Dad picked Tuyet up, ignoring the mess, and carried her across the rice paddy. Tuyet looked down. There was no water and the blades were not long enough. It wasn't a rice paddy at all. Instead, it was some sort of plant that grew straight and close together. It made her sad to think that no rice would grow in front of the house she lived in. But she was curious about this new plant and yearned to touch it. Why were all the blades the same length?

When they got into the house, Tuyet breathed in the fresh smell of lemongrass, which made her think of a time before the orphanage. The inside was open and cheerful, with white walls and colorful furniture and pictures. The floor was covered with a shaggy gold carpet. It felt homier than the stark white of Surrey Place, with its smell of bleach.

Dad set Tuyet down in the bathroom and left. Mom

came in and filled the tub with water. She squirted in some liquid from a bottle, and sweet-smelling bubbles immediately appeared. Tuyet frowned in confusion. She had always bathed herself with a basin of water and a rag. At Surrey Place, she showered to keep clean. Why did they think she needed this huge amount of water?

Mom helped her slip out of her dirty clothing, and then she motioned for Tuyet to get into the tub.

Tuyet reached into the tub and scooped up a hand-ful of the soapy water to show Mom how she could clean herself without getting into the tub. Mom shook her head. She lifted Tuyet up and placed her in the water.

At first, Tuyet was frightened, but the warm bubbly water felt wonderful, and it soothed her weak foot. She began to relax.

Mom helped her wash thoroughly, from the tips of her fingers to the bottoms of her toes. When Tuyet thought she was finished, Mom filled a bowl with the sudsy water. She held it over her own head to demon-strate what she was going to do. Tuyet nodded. She tilted her head back and felt the warm water spill all over her scalp and down her shoulders. Mom squirted out another liquid into the palm of her hand and worked it into Tuyet's scalp. The soap had a light, clean, and fresh scent.

Beth came in with a hand mirror. When Tuyet saw what she looked like with a mound of white foamy bubbles on her head, she laughed out loud. Mom rinsed it all out with fresh water from the tap and then she helped Tuyet out of the tub.

Tuyet had no clothing except for the dirty outfit from Surrey Place, so Mom wrapped her in a towel. Beth brought in some of her clothing for Tuyet to try on, but Tuyet was much taller and thinner than Beth. Nothing fit.

Mom got one of her own t-shirts and pulled it over Tuyet's head. The end of the shirt came down below Tuyet's knees. Mom knotted it so that it fit better.

"We're going to have to take you shopping," she said.

Beth loaned her a pair of underwear. Dad found some warm woolen socks that were stretchy enough to fit over Tuyet's weak foot without hurting it.

Lara stood in the doorway and chatted away, smiling. It didn't seem to matter that Tuyet had no idea what she said. Once Tuyet was dressed, Lara clasped one hand and Beth took the other. The three girls walked downstairs to the kitchen.

Mom sat Tuyet down at the table, put a piece of cloth on her lap, and set a bowl in front of her. It was filled with green leaves with a dollop of thick, dark orange liquid in the middle. After being sick over the crackers, Tuyet wasn't hungry. But that didn't matter—nothing put in front of her would ever go to waste.

Lara and Beth sat on either side of Tuyet, and Mom gave them each a bowl and cloth, as well. Dad put Aaron in a high chair and gave him a bowl of the greens but without the orange liquid on it. Dad was preparing other food over at the stove and Mom went over to help him.

Tuyet was about to pick up one of the green leaves with her fingers. But she stopped and peeked over at Lara and Beth, who had picked up a pronged instrument that did not look like chopsticks.

"It's a fork," said Beth, holding hers up to Tuyet. "Here's how to use it." She speared a few of the orange-doused leaves with the fork and shoved them into her mouth.

"Mmmm," said Beth. "I love Catalina dressing."

Lara held her fork with her fist and concentrated on her bowl. Aaron had another method. He grabbed the leaves one at a time with his fingertips and stuffed them in his mouth.

Tuyet picked up her fork and held it with her fist. She tried to push the sharp prongs into the leaves but it felt too awkward. She set the instrument down and held the bowl to her mouth. She opened her mouth wide and, with her fingers, guided a few leaves coated with the Catalina dressing on her tongue.

Tuyet's mouth was filled with the vilest taste she had ever experienced. The Catalina dressing had a horrible slimy texture, and it was oddly sweet and sour at the same time. She could feel the remnants of the crackers rise up in her throat. But she chewed slowly and swallowed the disgusting slime down.

There was still a lot more in her bowl. She took to

the chore bravely, one awful mouthful at a time. There was no way she could let this family know that she hated their food.

Mom brought a steaming container to the table and set it down. She regarded Tuyet's empty salad bowl and the expression on the girl's face.

"Don't eat it if you don't like it," said Mom.

Dad and Mom brought more covered containers and bigger flat dishes to the table. Then Mom opened the covered containers and filled each plate with some of the contents. She set one of the plates in front of Tuyet, who examined it. A piece of something pale brown, some yellow roundish things, and a scoop of white rice.

Tuyet's heart leapt at the sight of the rice. Holding the plate up, she shoveled the rice into her mouth with her fingers. She ate every last grain. The rice appeared to settle her stomach, so Tuyet picked up one of the yellow round things. It was slightly sweet and Tuyet liked the taste, but she didn't think she'd be able to eat them all. She picked up the brown piece of food—it looked like fish—and took a bite. It had a similar texture to the fish served at the orphanage, but it was tougher and bland. In the airplane, all the children were fed a broth with rice in it; sometimes there were chunks in it like this. One of the workers who spoke Vietnamese had told Tuyet it was called *chicken*. Tuyet took another bite.

All of a sudden, her stomach started churning. The last thing she wanted to do was to throw up again! While the others concentrated on their dinner, Tuyet took the piece of chicken and hid it in her sock.

Lara pointed at the yellow round things still on Tuyet's plate. "Corn," said Lara. "Mmmm."

Tuyet looked at the corn on her plate. Lara was right. It did taste good, but she was too full. She scooped up a handful of kernels and dropped them into her sock.

"My, you're a good eater," said Mom when she saw Tuyet's empty plate.

Once the children were finished, Dad took them back upstairs to the bathroom. He handed Tuyet a small pink stick with bristles on one end. She examined the stick carefully, not knowing what to do with it. Beth and Lara applied a smear of white paste onto their brushes from a tube and wet them with cold water from the sink. Beth looked into the bathroom mirror and bared her teeth. Lara giggled. Beth put the bristled end of the brush into her mouth and began to wash her teeth with it.

Tuyet understood. At the orphanage, they would use a bit of salt on a finger and clean their teeth with that. Tuyet picked up the tube and squeezed some paste on her brush. But when she put the brush in her mouth, her eyes widened in surprise. The paste did not taste at all like salt; it was an explosion of flavor. As she brushed, her mouth filled up with peppermint foam. She would have swallowed it down, but Beth and Lara spit the minty foam out into the sink and rinsed their brushes with water. Tuyet did the same.

There was so much to learn!

"Come see your bedroom," said the girls in unison, each tugging at one of her hands.

Tuyet let Beth and Lara pull her to a door across the hallway. Mom and Dad were close behind with Aaron.

Lara pushed open the door. "For you."

Tuyet stepped in. Along the wall sat a waist-height sleeping area covered with pink, soft material and topped with a puffy rectangle decorated with flowers.

Her doll, freshly cleaned, was propped up on the bed. Handled compartments were tucked into a tall wooden box that stood against another wall.

The elevated sleeping area was big enough for all the children, thought Tuyet. She looked down at the floor. A nice soft rug.

Tuyet understood now. This was the place where she would sleep. But why were they all standing around and smiling at her?

Mom walked into the room, picked up the doll, and put it into Tuyet's hand. Then she pulled down the fabric on the elevated sleeping area and pretended to get in under the fabric. She motioned for Tuyet to get in.

"This is your very own bed," said Mom. Then she pointed to Tuyet's feet.

It was time to take off her socks.

Slowly Tuyet pulled down her socks and slipped them off her feet. Mom, using hand gestures, indicated that her socks should be put in a small basket in the corner. Tuyet obeyed, carefully lowering each sock into the basket.

Nobody saw the hidden food.

Relieved, Tuyet climbed up into bed and hugged her doll tight. She marveled at the softness of the mattress and the fluffiness of the pillow. She was used to sleeping flat on the floor. She put her head down on the pillow. Mom pulled the material up over Tuyet's shoulders and tucked it in around her.

Mom bent down and kissed Tuyet on the cheek. Tuyet thrilled at the touch. Dad, holding Aaron, leaned over and kissed her, too.

"Good night, dear Tuyet," he said.

Aaron patted her cheek with his chubby hand. And Lara kissed her on the forehead.

Mom lifted Beth up to the bed so that her face hovered over Tuyet's.

"Good night, sister," she said, and gave Tuyet a smacking wet kiss right on the lips.

Tuyet smiled. She loved all the contact with these new people. She hoped they liked her. Maybe they wouldn't send her back to Surrey Place after all.

But then they left the room.

Mom clicked off the light and closed the door.

Tuyet was plunged into darkness.

Chapter Eight
The Darkness

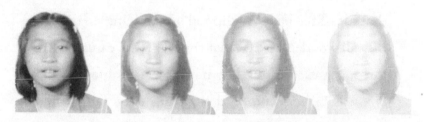

8-1

Tuyet's passport photographs

Tuyet waited for the door to open again and for the other children to join her. She waited and waited and waited. The door stayed closed. She was alone in the dark.

Tuyet clung to her doll and closed her eyes. But sleep wouldn't come. The bed was too big for just one person. As she pulled the soft covers up to her face,

Tuyet tried not to think of all the times when she had been left on her own. That other mother, who stopped visiting. The white van that took her away from the special boy. Linh, who had left her for that family. They all came back to Tuyet, like a nightmare she was helpless to stop. Would she always be alone?

Would she ever be important to a family that already had two girls and a boy?

Tuyet set her doll down. Swinging her legs over the side of the bed, she slipped out and limped over to the tall wooden box against the wall. She caressed the top and was comforted by its smooth coolness. If the box was in her room, did that mean the family had given it to her? What a huge possession. Her hand brushed down the front of the box and her fingertips landed on the first handle. She pulled. A drawer slid out, bigger than the boxes that had carried the babies to Canada. Tuyet pushed herself up as tall as she could and felt inside. Nothing there.

She limped to the clothing hamper, took out her socks, and carried them back to the top drawer. Holding the socks by the toes, she gave them a shake. Kernels of corn and the piece of chicken fell out. When her socks were empty, she pushed the food with her fingertips into the back corners of the drawer.

If they forgot to feed her, at least she would have something to eat.

Tuyet stepped to the window and drew back the curtains. The stars filled the dark sky—so many that she could not count them. So bright and sparkling. So beautiful. It was the best thing about her new country, seeing the stars, knowing they weren't bombs or helicopters and couldn't hurt her.

She left the curtains open and climbed back into bed. She hugged her doll and thought of Surrey Place, where she, Linh, and the babies had slept so close to one other.

Tuyet wondered if the others slept by themselves. She walked to her door and opened it a crack. She could hear rhythmic breathing coming from one of the rooms and a gentle snore from another. She pulled the door open wider—

Squeak!

Tuyet started. She held her breath. Had she woken anyone?

But the rhythmic breathing continued.

If she limped down the hallway, she was sure to make noise. She had only one choice. Tucking her doll into the neck of her shirt, she got down onto the floor and dragged herself silently along the hallway until she reached the first door. She pulled herself up with care and turned the doorknob slowly. Terrified of another *squeak*, she held her breath and pushed the door open just far enough to peek inside.

The room was similar to hers, but this one had a bed on either side. Between the beds was a window, the curtain opened slightly. On the floor sat a small rug, just like in her room. In one bed, Tuyet could make out the form of Beth snuggled up under the covers, her long hair splayed out over the pillow. In the other was Lara, deep in sleep on her back, her arms flung above her head.

Tuyet longed to sleep in this room with the two girls. Their closeness would comfort her. The sound of their breathing would lull her nightmares away. She softly closed the door and crawled to the next bedroom. This one was smaller. Tuyet could see the barred sides of Aaron's crib. He slept, curled in a ball, in one corner of the crib.

The low snoring noise got a little louder as Tuyet made her way to the end of the hall. At the convent, one of the older nuns snored, so the sound did not frighten Tuyet. If anything, she found it a comfort. She gingerly pushed open the door and poked her head in. Mom and Dad were sound asleep in their bed.

Tuyet closed the door as gently as she could and headed back along the hall. But instead of passing Beth and Lara's room, she stopped for a moment and leaned against the door. How she longed to go into that room and sleep on the rug between them.

It was so frightening to think of sleeping alone. But she didn't want to disappoint this family. She had to make herself agreeable so they would never think of sending her back.

Tuyet returned to her own room.

She knew she would never sleep if she got back into the soft bed, so she hugged her doll and curled up on the rug. She'd wake up early and get into the bed.

No one would know the difference.

Chapter Nine
Dad

The first bits of daylight warmed Tuyet's face. In her dreams, she was still in the orphanage, sleeping on the wood slat floor. She opened her eyes. She was on a rug on the floor. She sat up and felt her cheek. It was rippled with the impression of a soft rug instead of wooden slats.

It all came back to her in a rush. She was alone, but this room, the too-soft bed, the chest of drawers where she'd hidden extra food—they were all her very own. And the stars…

She limped to the window. The morning sky was a crisp bright blue with tufted clouds, and the ground was carpeted in green. There were objects on the green, but she didn't quite know what they were.

The doorknob was turning! Tuyet grabbed her doll and jumped into the bed just as the door squeaked open. Mom walked in, smiling, carrying Tuyet's freshly laundered pants and her sweater from Surrey Place. But as soon as Mom saw Tuyet's face, her smile disappeared.

"What happened to your cheek?"

Mom placed the clothing on the dresser and sat down on the bed. She touched the spot on Tuyet's cheek where the rug had made its mark. Tuyet was scared. Would she be punished for sleeping on the floor? The woman didn't seem angry, but she wasn't happy either.

All at once, Mom wrapped her arms around Tuyet, drawing her in close. It felt so good to be held. It almost felt like being safe.

Just then, Lara and Beth tumbled into the room, hair awry, still in their pajamas.

"Good morning, Tuyet," said Lara.

"Morning, sister," said Beth. "I heard you outside our room last night."

Tuyet didn't know what the girls were saying, but she could see right away that Beth's words had caught Mom's attention.

"Tuyet was in the hallway last night?" Mom asked.

"She was outside our door for a long time," said Beth. "I don't think she likes sleeping alone."

Mom patted the bed. "Let's all give Tuyet a hug."

The girls climbed up onto the bed. Soon they were all over Tuyet, hugging and tickling until they all dissolved in a fit of giggles.

Mom looked at her wristwatch. "Girls," she said, "it's time to get dressed. We're going to be late for church."

Beth grabbed Lara's hand and the two girls ran to their own bedroom.

Mom pointed to the freshly laundered clothing that she had set on top of the dresser and hurried out.

Tuyet put on her Surrey Place clothes and went down the hallway to the bathroom. Lara and Beth were dressed and at the sink, brushing their teeth. Mom was kneeling beside the tub, bathing Aaron.

Tuyet couldn't help Beth and Lara brush their

teeth, but she was determined to show Mom that she could be a good worker. Tuyet knelt beside Mom at the side of the tub and tried to edge her out of the way. She grabbed the face cloth from Mom's hand.

Mom took the face cloth back. "You are my daughter," she said. "Not my helper."

Tuyet was confused. Why was she here if not to help with the children?

Mom pointed to Beth and Lara and made motions like brushing her teeth. Tuyet stood up and stepped over to the sink. At least she could understand Mom some of the time.

Tuyet followed Beth and Lara to the kitchen, where Dad was setting out bowls, spoons, milk, and a mysterious box. Tuyet sat in a chair between the two younger girls. Beth poured what looked like small pebbles from the box into her bowl, and passed the box to Tuyet, who copied her then handed the box to Lara. Lara poured milk all over the pebbles, so Tuyet did the same.

"Cheerios," said Lara, picking up her spoon and pointing it at the box.

Tuyet examined her spoon. It looked like a more practical tool than the pronged instrument from the evening before. She dipped the spoon into her bowl, filled it, and tasted the pebbles. They were crunchy and sweet—much better than Catalina dressing!

The spoon was slowing her down, so Tuyet picked up her bowl and slurped down her breakfast. She gave a loud burp to show that she appreciated the good food. Dad looked over in surprise, but he didn't comment.

Tuyet had just finished her breakfast when Mom arrived, wearing a fancy outfit and carrying Aaron on her hip. She didn't sit down for breakfast.

"We're going to be late for church," she said.

Beth and Lara quickly finished their Cheerios and got up from the table, taking their bowls and spoons with them and depositing them in the kitchen sink.

Tuyet stood up to follow the girls, but Mom put up her hand and said, "No. We need to buy you shoes on Monday. You can come to church with us next week."

Tuyet didn't understand.

Mom pointed to her own feet, and then to Tuyet's. "No shoes," she said.

Tuyet had no shoes. She understood that much.

Mom kissed Dad on the cheek. Then she carried Aaron out the door. Beth and Lara followed.

Tuyet hobbled to the front door as quickly as she could. She reached the handle and was almost outside when Dad put his hand on her shoulder.

"No," he said.

Tuyet looked up at him in confusion. He didn't seem angry. The two of them stood together in the doorway and watched Mom drive off with the children.

Tuyet and Dad were left by themselves.

So it *was* too good to be true. This woman didn't want to be her mom after all. Beth, Lara, and Aaron weren't going to be her family. She wasn't going back to Surrey Place. Instead, they were going someplace else and she was staying here. But why had they left Dad behind, as well?

Maybe Tuyet had misunderstood. Maybe Dad wasn't a part of the family. Maybe dads didn't really exist in this country, either.

Tuyet felt like sitting down on the floor and bursting into tears, but what would this man do to her if she cried? Feeling like her feet were made of heavy stones, she headed slowly back to the kitchen. Two bowls and spoons were left on the table. She picked them up and carried them to the sink.

Dad filled the sink with soapy water. This was something she could do. She placed her hands on Dad's hip and pushed, trying to get him to move away from the sink. He looked down at her and smiled, but he didn't move over.

Dad washed all the dishes, rinsed them, and put them on the drying rack. When he was finished, he took two towels out of the drawer and handed her one. He dried one of the bowls and set it in the cupboard. She dried one bowl and handed it to him.

"Thank you," he said.

But soon they were done. How could she prove herself useful now?

Tuyet stood warily as Dad went to the closet. He brought out the white rubber boots. Her heart sank. So she was going back to Surrey Place, after all. But how would they get there without the car? Tuyet hoped that she wouldn't have to walk. It seemed a long distance.

Dad motioned for her to join him by the big window, and held her steady as she stepped into the tall boots. He slipped his own feet into a pair of shoes and pushed on the giant window.

It slid open! It wasn't a window, but a glass door.

Dad took Tuyet's hand and the two of them stepped outside onto a wooden porch. The air was cooler than the day before and a shiver ran through Tuyet. Dad went back inside and came out with a sweater. He popped it over her head and she slipped her arms into the sleeves, which were so long, they went down practically to her knees. Dad rolled the sleeves up until her hands peeked out. The sweater was cozy and warm. She looked up at Dad and smiled.

He stepped down onto the green carpet and Tuyet followed him. She wanted to touch the green stems, but her boots were so tall that it was hard to crouch down. Dad sat right down on the green and patted the spot beside him. Tuyet sat, her giant boots splayed out in front of her. She placed her palm down on the green and felt its cold dampness.

"*Grass*," said Dad. He pulled out one blade and handed it to her.

Tuyet examined it carefully. It was a perfect, tiny knife of green.

Dad ran his hand through the grass as if he were looking for something.

"There's one," he said, pulling up a broad piece of grass. He held it flat between his two thumbs and brought it to his lips. He blew, making a shrill, whistling noise.

At first Tuyet was startled by the noise, but Dad did it again, and she found the noise so absurd that she giggled. He showed her how he held the blade. Tuyet held hers between her thumbs. She brought it to her lips and blew, but it didn't work. Dad combed his fingers through the grass and found another broad blade and handed it to her.

It took her a few tries, but soon she was making as much noise as Dad. He laughed out loud and she grinned. Maybe it would be okay, after all.

Dad stood up and held out his hand to help Tuyet to her feet. He pointed to one of the objects that she had seen from her bedroom window. It was a metal framework with pairs of rope hanging down, a wooden slat between each pair of ropes.

"*Swing*," Dad said.

Tuyet stared at him in confusion. Dad sat on one of the seats. He pushed off with his feet and swung back and forth. Tuyet couldn't help but smile. It seemed like such an odd thing to do. Dad hopped off the swing, picked her up, and placed her on it, showing her where to hold the ropes so that she would be steady. She gripped the rope. It was an odd sensation, like floating in the air. Dad stood behind her and gave her a gentle push.

Tuyet smiled.

Dad pushed her a bit more. The swing rocked gently back and forth, and Tuyet felt the wind on her face. The sky and the grass sped up before her. It seemed like such a wasteful thing to do—sitting, feeling the swing go back and forth, watching the world speed up. It didn't seem to have any purpose at all. Tuyet did not feel useful sitting there.

But she could have stayed on it for hours.

It was ... fun!

Tuyet was so entranced that she didn't notice her hands were starting to turn blue with the cold. But Dad saw. He put his hands on the rope and steadied the swing until it stopped. He lifted her off and held her in his arms. She clung to him and felt his warmth.

Dad carried Tuyet around the yard. He pointed at objects and told her what their English names were—*sandbox, monkey bars, back porch, fence*. It seemed there was no end to the marvels of the backyard.

"Play," he said, holding one arm out wide.

They walked up the porch steps and through the sliding glass door. Dad set her back on her feet and pointed to the table. She sat on one of the chairs. Dad left the room. Within moments, he was back, carrying a worn cardboard box. He upended the contents onto the table. Wooden blocks.

Dad and Tuyet spent the rest of the morning building tall towers and knocking them down.

Tuyet heard the sound of a car pulling into the driveway.

"Mom, Aaron, Beth, and Lara are home," said Dad.

Tuyet ran to the front door. It was true! They had come back! Beth was first through the door, with Lara close behind her.

"Want to play outside?" she asked Tuyet.

Tuyet knew *play*. She knew *outside*. She nodded.

là tình yêu đẹp xinh mến chúa yêu người là
điều răn chúa anh em hãy tôn thờ những
lời ngài đã ban.

Bài ca (8)
Em viết chữ y

Em viết chữ g, em viết chữ ê, em thêm chữ u, em
lồng đa yêu yêu cha là mẹ, yêu ông là yêu bố, yêu cô
bác gần xa em yêu là yêu.

Bài ca (9)

Đám cưới trên đường quê hương
Ô, ô sáng hôm nay trên quê hương tôi, quê hương
sinh sinh quê hương hữu tình, quê hương xinh xinh quê
hương hòa bình đường làm sao trắng xanh vàng tím
đẹp làm sao bướm bay chầm chậm đàn chim non réo
lên ngọn tre khăn màu xổ áo màu hồng đi bà con
đến xem mùa cưới chân hài công tay đủ hồng ra
mà xem mới thấy được một nhiên vui anh đi mời tình
tôi đi anh đi xem người ta hô cưới nhau rồi.
Ô, ô sáng hôm nay tôi ra tôi xem cô dâu non non
nhụn nhắng mỹ mèo cô dâu son non nhụn nhắng mặt
mãi, chã nhà ai có ông về qui chã nhà ai có cô dâu
hiền cô thầy cô to con lằng quai tôi mười mầm cá o
đầy buồn ra mà xem mới thấy được một nhiệm vui
em đi mời tình tôi đi em đi xem người ta hô cưới
nhau rồi.

Bài ca (10)
Cái nhà

Cái nhà là nhà của ta ông cô ông cha lập ra chúng
con hãy gìn giữ lấy muôn năm lấy m nước lau nhà.

A sample of Tuyet's Vietnamese writing

Chapter Ten
Joy

That afternoon, Tuyet learned about making shapes in the sandbox with damp sand and a pail. She hung from the monkey bar with both hands while Beth and Lara tumbled around her. One day she would be strong enough to follow them, but for now, she only cared about being part of the family. She didn't speak the same language yet, but they all seemed to communicate fine. It still felt odd to be playing with children instead of standing back and watching. But it was a good feeling.

She was pushing Lara on the swing when Dad stepped outside.

"Tuyet," he said. He motioned with his hand for her to come in.

Had she done something wrong? She steadied the swing and helped Lara down, then she trudged inside.

Her eyes took a few seconds to adjust to the light indoors. Three people sat at the kitchen table—a man,

10-1   *Tuyet with Linh, May 1975*

a woman, and a girl. She blinked. She had seen this man and woman before. She looked at the girl.

It couldn't possibly be. She rubbed her eyes and blinked again.

"Linh?"

The girl jumped out of the chair so quickly that she nearly upended it. She ran to Tuyet and wrapped her arms around her.

Tuyet hugged her friend and wept and wept.

"How did you find me?" she asked when she could speak again.

"It was a care worker," said Linh. "Someone told our parents about our friendship. We live close enough to visit."

"Come on," said Tuyet. "I want you to meet Beth and Lara. And you've got to see the big outside with all the play things."

Linh stayed the entire afternoon. Tuyet was so happy that her heart felt like it would burst.

When it was time for bed, Tuyet was so filled with contentment that she thought she might be able to sleep on her own. The happy memories of the day would drive out her fears. But when she went into her bedroom, something had changed. The bed was bare.

Tuyet turned. Beth stood in the doorway, a grin on her face.

"Come on," she said. "We have another surprise for you."

Tuyet followed Beth into the girls' room. Lara sat cross-legged on her own bed. On the floor between the two beds were Tuyet's sheets, blankets, and pillow—made up like her own special bed.

"You can sleep with us as long as you want," said Lara.

That night, Tuyet slept on the floor between her two sisters, wrapped in the comforting sound of their rhythmic breathing.

In the middle of the night, she woke up and slipped out of bed. She looked out the window. They were still there, sparkling down on her.

So many stars. Too many to count.

10-2   *Beth, Tuyet, Aaron, and Lara,*
first day of school, 1978

ONE STEP AT A TIME:

A Vietnamese Child Finds Her Way

To Beth, Lara, and Aaron

Chapter One
The Night Before

Tuyet burrowed into her nest of pillows and covers on the throw rug between Beth and Lara's beds. She had a room of her own, but Tuyet still found comfort in the sound of her new sisters' rhythmic breathing. Her mom and dad had decided it would be all right to sleep on the floor, at least until she was ready to sleep on her own.

If she was very still, she could hear the tick-tick of a clock down the hallway, along with Dad's heavy snores. She kept her eyes tightly closed and hugged her Holly Hobbie doll, but sleep would not come. In just a few hours, Tuyet's life would change forever.

Instead of sleep, the memories came…

A giant BOOM…*fire and smoke.*
Pain.
Her back and scalp on fire. Hair aflame and smoking.
Doctors hovering over her with strange instruments.
The whup whup whup *of helicopters above.*
Moans from other injured people in cots close by…

Tuyet thought she had buried those memories for good.
But ever since her ankle surgery had been scheduled, the
terrors were back, keeping her awake nearly every night.
She pulled the covers over her head and squeezed her eyes
shut. The images wouldn't go away. Still clutching her
doll, Tuyet pushed off the covers and sat up. Four-year-old
Beth and three-year-old Lara were sleeping peacefully.

Tuyet balanced on her one good foot and peeked
though the curtains at the night sky.

No helicopters, no fire, no smoke.

This wasn't the orphanage in Saigon. She didn't
live in Vietnam anymore.

Tuyet left the curtain open, just enough to let the moonlight in. She looked down at her legs. The right one was strong and straight, and her foot pointed in the right direction. But her left leg was no larger than Lara's, and it was weak. Her ankle turned inward, making her foot useless. She had to limp on the bone of her ankle to get around. She'd push on her knee with the palm of her hand to make her injured leg move. She'd gotten used to the build-up of calluses on her knee and hand, and she hardly noticed the constant pain in her ankle anymore.

What would her left leg and ankle look like after the surgery? It was hard to imagine.

How much would the surgery hurt? That's what frightened her the most. She could handle the pain she already had, but she did not want more of it.

Tuyet tugged the curtains closed then limped to the bedroom door and opened it, listening for the sound of Dad's snores. His snoring was usually a comfort, but tonight it wasn't enough.

Tuyet held her doll in the crook of her arm as she silently shuffled down the hallway, first poking her head into Aaron's room. He was safe in his crib. When she reached her parents' bedroom, Tuyet pushed open the door. They were in bed, bathed in shadows, fast asleep.

How she longed to crawl under the covers between them. Maybe the memories would stay away. But she didn't want to bother them. She got down onto the floor and pulled herself under their bed, huddling into a ball with her doll safe within her arms, little bits of dust tickling her nose. The space beneath the bed was just the perfect size for her. Dad's snoring was comfortingly loud.

Tuyet fell into a dreamless sleep.

In the morning, beams of sunlight woke her as they lit the floor around her parents' bed. She pulled herself out from under the bed and shuffled quietly back to her own spot between her two sisters. She closed her eyes and pretended to sleep, pleased at the thought of the secret safe place she had found to keep the memories away. If only she could stay there forever. If only she didn't have to go to the hospital today.

Beth and Lara woke, but Tuyet kept her eyes closed. She could feel a warm hand on her shoulder. "Wake up,

1-1   *The Morris family. From left, Lara, John,*
                                       Tuyet, Beth, Dorothy, Aaron

Sis," said Lara. "It's your operation day."

Tuyet squeezed her eyes shut. Maybe if she pretended to be asleep, she wouldn't have to go.

She heard her sisters leave the bedroom, then heard morning noises down the hallway. Dad came in and knelt beside her.

"Time to get up, Tuyet."

She kept her eyes closed tight.

Mom's footsteps stopped at the doorway. "Why don't we let her sleep a bit longer, John?"

Tuyet didn't understand all the words, but whatever Mom said, it worked. Dad got up and left. A little while later, she heard the car pull out of the driveway. Maybe he decided not to take her to the hospital after all.

But an hour later, Dad came back. "It's time for us to go."

Chapter Two
Red Shoes

Tuyet sat in the front seat of the car with her doll on her lap and Dad in the driver's seat. Beth and Lara solemnly waved good-bye from the front window of the house. Aaron stood between them, his two hands firmly planted on the glass.

Mom crouched beside the open door of the car so that she was eye level with Tuyet. "You are my brave girl," she said, lightly kissing Tuyet on the cheek.

Mom closed the car door.

Dad turned on the ignition and put the car in reverse. "You are going to be okay," he said.

Tuyet didn't know the meaning of the words, but

they sounded reassuring. What was about to happen was still unknown, but right now she cherished what she had—her own mom and dad, two sisters and a brother, a home of her own. No matter what happened about her ankle, she had her own family and her own home. That was what she cared about most.

As they drove in silence, Tuyet looked down at her special pair of red shoes. Just the sight of them reassured Tuyet that she was loved. Tuyet smiled to herself, remembering.

When she had met her family for the first time, she had been wearing rain boots. Tuyet could barely walk in the white boots, which were many sizes too large. But it was raining outside, and the care workers couldn't find anything else for her to wear. She couldn't leave the building in Toronto barefoot.

Everyone else in the Morris family had a pair of shoes. Even Aaron, who was still a baby, had shoes! Beth's favorite shoes were beautiful shiny red ones with a strap across the top. Tuyet loved gliding her finger over their smooth, glossy surfaces. Lara's favorites were bright pink running shoes. Not only were they pretty, but they had tough, rubbery soles that were perfect for running and kicking a ball. Tuyet longed to run and kick a ball. She could barely walk in the big white boots. But she knew that even if she had shoes like everybody else, she still wouldn't be able to kick a ball. She'd need two good feet inside the shoes to be able to do that.

Mom knew that Tuyet wanted shoes of her own instead of the ugly white boots. Tuyet had only been in Brantford for a couple of days when Mom took her shoe shopping at the huge Woolco store. Tuyet looked at the racks and racks of shoes in every imaginable style and every possible size. She couldn't believe that stores could be so big. Tuyet limped through the aisles, wishing she could wear a pair of shoes like other people. Mom followed behind, her brow knitted in thought.

Tuyet picked out a pair of red shiny shoes. They were just like Beth's.

Mom held onto the shoes, but they kept on looking. Suddenly, Mom's eyes lit up. She grabbed something from a rack above Tuyet's eye level and then motioned for Tuyet to sit in a chair.

Mom knelt down and drew off the ugly rubber boots. Onto the right foot, she slipped a red shoe. She pulled the strap tight across the top of Tuyet's foot and fastened the buckle.

Tuyet straightened out her good knee and admired her healthy foot. The shoe looked beautiful from every angle. If only the matching shoe would fit onto her tiny left foot with the bent ankle, but of course she knew that wasn't possible.

She smiled at Mom to hide the heaviness in her heart. She knew how hard Mom was trying, and that in itself felt good.

Mom grinned mischievously and showed Tuyet the other item. It was red as well, but it looked like a small sweater. Mom gently drew off the other rubber boot and carefully pulled the red knitted thing over Tuyet's tiny foot, making sure not to hurt her bent ankle, drawing it up to her calf.

Once it was on, Tuyet realized that it wasn't a sweater, but a soft slipper with a sturdy leather sole. She looked down at both of her feet and nearly wept. For the first time in her life, she owned a pair of shoes, and they were red, too!

Dad went over a bump in the road and Tuyet's thoughts about that shopping trip fled from her mind. She remembered that she was on the way to the hospital. She was going to have surgery. She looked back down at her special red shoes. That made her feel better.

Tuyet gazed out the window and realized that they were already on the highway. She watched Dad as he concentrated on the road. He turned to her briefly and smiled.

"It's going to be fine," he said.

Tuyet thought back to the day she first found out she was going to have surgery. It had been only a few days after Mom had bought her the shoes.

Mom wouldn't let her help with the chores and wouldn't let her help with Aaron.

"Scoot," said Mom. "Go play."

Tuyet tried hard at this new skill, this *playing*, which seemed so important to her parents. She and her sisters and brother would play on the swing set in the backyard, and they would make mounds in the sandbox. And that was fun. But sometimes Tuyet would sit on the front step. Most of the children on the street were young like her sisters and brother, but there were two boys her age next door, and sometimes they'd kick a ball back and forth to each other. She was sure they didn't even know that she existed. How she longed to play with them, to kick a ball. But even with her new shoes, Tuyet could not kick a ball. She could not run.

So just as she had done in the Saigon orphanage, Tuyet sat and watched instead.

One evening, Tuyet was sitting on the front lawn when an unfamiliar car pulled into the Morris driveway. A Vietnamese woman stepped out. Tuyet began to shake as she struggled to her feet. Was the woman here to take Tuyet away?

"Good afternoon, Son Thi Anh Tuyet," the woman

said in Vietnamese. "My name is Mrs. Nguyen. I am here to visit your parents. Can you let them know that I am here?"

"Go away!" Tuyet shouted in Vietnamese. She expected the woman to be angered by her rudeness, but the woman's face remained serene.

Mrs. Nguyen walked up to the front door and knocked.

In a panic, Tuyet limped away as fast as she could. Looking for a place to hide, she crept behind a bush in the neighbor's yard.

Then she peeked through the branches. Mom had opened the door.

"Please make her go," Tuyet prayed.

But Mom was smiling! The woman followed Mom into the house.

Tuyet waited behind the bush, her heart sinking.

Was there something she had done to anger Mom and Dad?

Tuyet had been so sure that she was part of the Morris family now. Mom wouldn't have bought her the special red shoes unless she was family, so why was this woman here? Tuyet did not want to go back to the or-phanage. She was a Morris now. This was home.

Dad opened the front door and stepped out. "Tuyet!" he called. "Where are you?"

Tuyet crouched down.

It didn't take Dad long to find her. He picked her up gently and carried her inside. Tuyet was numb with fear.

He sat down on the sofa beside Mom, his arms still wrapped protectively around Tuyet's waist.

"Child, I am here to help you," said Mrs. Nguyen in Vietnamese.

Tuyet buried her head into her father's chest. She could feel Mom's hand caressing her shoulder.

"Your parents asked me to translate some things for them."

Tuyet did not want a translation. She could not stop trembling.

Dad hugged her more tightly.

Mom said, "We love you, Tuyet. Everything will be fine."

"Most important," said Mrs. Nguyen. "You are not going back to Vietnam."

Tuyet held her herself very still. Had she heard right?

"This is your home. These are your parents. That will not change."

Tuyet loosened her grip on Dad's neck and turned her head so she could see Mrs. Nguyen from the corner of her eye. The woman seemed calm and kind. She did not look like a liar.

Tuyet slipped off Dad's lap and snuggled in to the narrow spot on the sofa between Mom and Dad. Mom grabbed one of her hands and gave it a reassuring squeeze. Dad held her other hand in both of his.

"You want to be able to play like other children, don't you?" asked Mrs. Nguyen.

It was as if Mrs. Nguyen had reached inside Tuyet's heart. More than anything, this is what Tuyet wanted, but she knew it was not possible. She looked down at her shoes. She couldn't answer Mrs. Nguyen.

"Your parents need to take you to the doctor, to see what can be done to strengthen and straighten your left ankle."

"I don't want a doctor," said Tuyet.

"You need a doctor," said the woman.

"A doctor will cut open my ankle."

"Only to put it back together in a better way. Don't you want to try, Son Thi Anh Tuyet?"

"Will I be able to walk?" asked Tuyet.

"Maybe," said Mrs. Nguyen.

"Will I be able to kick a ball?"

"One step at a time," said Mrs. Nguyen with a smile.

This plan to have her ankle straightened felt like reaching for the stars. Tuyet had been eager when the surgery seemed like a dream in the future, but now that the day was upon her, she was having second thoughts.

Stars weren't meant to be touched. Maybe her ankle was never meant to be straight.

Tuyet looked out the car window and tried not to think.

3-1

McMaster University Medical Centre,
opened in 1972

Chapter Three
The Hospital

Dad parked the car. He carried Tuyet into the huge concrete building.

Tuyet tried to calm herself. She thought of the frightening experiences that had transformed her life.

The nuns at the orphanage. They had terrified her at first, but they protected her from the bombs and bullets and they gave her food and a place to sleep.

The giant airplane. Tuyet had covered her eyes at the sight of it. But she made herself go inside, and that huge flying building rescued her from the war. If she hadn't swallowed her fear, she might never have come to Canada.

She might never have found her new family...

Tuyet clutched her father's neck with one arm and

held her doll in the other as he carried her through the busy corridors of McMaster Hospital. She watched a woman pass by with a boy who was about her own age. They didn't notice her at all.

The boy did not look scared. If anything, he looked bored.

Tuyet looked at the faces of other people.

No one looked frightened.

Maybe this hospital really would straighten her ankle. Tuyet tried to appear calm as she and Dad got into the elevator. Dad pressed the number Three.

Three was not an unlucky number.

The doors opened up onto the brightly painted children's ward, with its floor-to-ceiling windows, but Tuyet was too numb to take in the details.

She didn't notice the playroom filled with child-sized furniture and boxes of toys, or the cartoon mural on the wall, or the huge see-through fish tank.

Tuyet thought they would let Dad stay with her, but instead they sent him home.

Tuyet trembled as a uniformed woman helped her remove her special red shoes and her socks. The nurse took away Tuyet's doll and helped her change into a plain cotton gown. The woman neatly folded Tuyet's bell-bottomed pants and new top that Mom had bought her. Then she lifted her onto a wheeled cot and motioned for Tuyet to lie down.

Tuyet felt so alone. So afraid.

She tried not to think of anything at all as a smiling man wheeled her into a stark white room with lots of shiny metal instruments and bright lights.

People with cotton masks over the bottom part of their faces gathered around her and spoke in soothing tones.

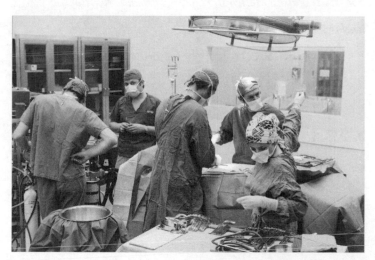

3-2

McMaster University Medical Centre operating room, circa 1975

Tuyet willed herself not to think of that other time in the hospital. *People weeping, helicopters overhead.* This would be different. This time she would have a family to go home to.

Warm hands steadied her forearm and she felt a faint prick, then a sensation of cold tingling under her skin. Her eyes went heavy.

A flash of memory—

She is lying on a sweat-drenched mat on the floor of a bamboo stilt house. Helicopters fly overhead, while the bang and crash of explosions make the ground tremble.

A woman hovers over her, cooling her forehead with a damp cloth, but it doesn't help. Pain spasms through her left leg. The woman holds a cup to her mouth, but the water dribbles down her chin.

Her throat is parched but she cannot swallow...

She hovers between wake and sleep.

She lies in the stilt house for days. The woman is always there, her eyes red from weeping. "I cannot help you, my daughter. Please do not die."

She is wracked with pain.

Strong sinewy arms lift her from the sweat-soaked mat. Her mother runs, carrying her, as bombs explode all round.

Another cot and other doctors. The spasms go away from her left leg, but she cannot get it to move anymore. Doctors send her weeping mother home.

A strange veiled woman in white carries Tuyet away from the hospital...to a building with many other children. Tuyet calls for her mother. She grows hoarse from crying.

Then she forgets.

Much later a woman visits. Is it her mother?

She visits once.

Twice.

Never again.

Tuyet shook the images out of her mind. That was in the past. It was a time of deep sadness. A time of belonging to no one. A time that she needed to forget.

Tuyet's tongue felt swollen and her throat was dry, but she felt no pain. This was strange in itself.

Tuyet could not remember a time without pain. Didn't everyone feel constant pain? It was just a part of living, after all.

She opened one eye and saw that she was no longer in the operating room. Instead she was propped up in a bed with rails along both sides. She opened her other eye. Holly Hobbie was tucked in beside her. Tuyet smiled. The doll reminded her of home, that she was Tuyet Morris now.

When she reached to hug her doll, something pulled at her left hand. A length of narrow plastic tubing was attached to the back of her hand with a bandage. Her eyes followed the length of tube to the other end, where it was attached to a clear plastic bag filled with fluid. The bag was hooked onto a tall metal pole. Fluid drip-dripped steadily from the plastic bag into the tubing.

A kind-looking woman wearing a flowered smock sat in a chair close to Tuyet's bed. She offered Tuyet a plastic glass with a straw and said something in English. Tuyet took a sip—fresh cold water—and was reassured to find that she could swallow it. The water felt so soothing on her tongue and throat that she would have drunk the whole glass, but the woman took it away from her after just two sips.

Tuyet looked down the length of the bed. The outline of both her legs was visible through the white cotton sheet. Her left leg, usually smaller, looked bigger now, and it was propped on a pillow. She reached out to touch it.

It felt like a rock.

She pulled back the sheet. From just below her knee to the tip of her toe, her leg was encased in what looked like a column of white cement. Even though there was nothing in her stomach except for those little sips of water, Tuyet felt as if she was about to throw up. She lay back against her pillow.

How would she ever be able to walk with this huge piece of cement weighing her down? Maybe it was all a nightmare. She closed her eyes and tried to make it go away.

Chapter Four
Black Button

Tuyet drifted in and out of sleep. Once, when she was barely awake, the woman in the flowered smock showed her a black button on the end of a long cord.

"If you need me, push this," she said, looping it securely around the bed rail.

Tuyet wished she knew what the woman was saying.

Another time, the woman woke her and helped her sit up. Tuyet felt dizzy and her head was heavy with sleep, but the woman gently helped Tuyet off the bed and guided her to the bathroom. Once Tuyet was finished and back in bed, the woman pointed to the button again.

"Push this if you need me."

And then Tuyet understood. If she needed to go to the bathroom, she should push the button and the woman would come back to assist her.

It was still dark outside, too early to be awake. Tuyet closed her eyes, but it was no use. She was wide awake. She closed her eyes again and tried to pretend that she was snuggled in her nest of pillows and blankets on the floor between Beth and Lara. But her spine sank down into the unfamiliar hospital mattress. She tried to shift her position, but the tubing in the back of her hand got in the way whenever she moved, and the cast was heavy and awkward. She tried to think of home, but the sounds were all wrong. Instead of Dad's snore, she could hear people speaking in low voices down the hallway and a faint *beep, beep, beep* of a machine in another room. No matter how hard she tried, she couldn't trick herself into feeling at home... but then...

She is back inside the giant airplane that will carry her away from Vietnam. The caregivers are frantic; they bring in more babies. Rows of cardboard boxes, all filled with hot, screaming babies. Sweat drips down her forehead and stings her eyes as she moves from box to box.

Her hand trembles as she reaches into a box to comfort a frightened infant.

"Soon you will be safe," she coos, hoping it isn't a lie.

A woman scoops Tuyet off the floor of the aircraft and sets her in a chair. She reaches for a seatbelt, but instead the woman pours wet cement on both of Tuyet's legs. It hardens in an instant. She cannot move.

She peers out the window of the airplane. Beth and Lara are on the tarmac, and their legs are in cement as well. Aaron sits on the hot pavement between them, screaming. He sounds just like the babies in the boxes.

Soon the airplane will be taking off. She has to warn them. If they don't get on the airplane, they will be left behind. She will never see them again!

Tuyet pounds on the window, but Beth and Lara don't see her. They are looking down at their cement legs—

Tuyet woke with a jolt. She looked around and saw that she was not on the airplane. She was in a hospital bed and only one leg had cement on it. Beth, Aaron, and Lara were safe at home, not in Vietnam. Tuyet knew it, but her heart was still pounding.

Her ankle throbbed and her bum felt tingly from lying in the same spot for so long. She tried shifting her weight, but it was impossible to get comfortable. She reached down to massage her ankle, but with the cast on, she couldn't get to the spot where it hurt.

Tuyet flopped back on her pillow, feeling trapped and frustrated. Hot tears spilled down her cheeks, which made her angry with herself. She took a deep breath and willed the pain away. But it was no use.

The whole thing was a big mistake. Had the doctors cut her leg open as they said they would, things would have been bad enough. But instead they had just covered her leg in cement. Before they started fooling around with her leg, at least she had been able to get around. Now she was trapped in this cast, and her leg hurt more than ever before. She should have been satisfied with what she already had instead of trying to reach for the stars.

She drifted off to sleep again, but stabbing pains woke her up. The pain would have been bearable with Dad and Mom there, but Tuyet was all alone. She tried to hold her feelings in, but still the tears coursed down her cheeks.

Desperate, Tuyet pushed the black button. She didn't have to go to the bathroom, but she needed to have someone close by.

A nurse rushed in. It wasn't the woman in the flowered smock. "What can I get you?" she asked.

Tuyet didn't want the nurse to see her cry. She turned her face to the pillow. The nurse sat down on the edge of the bed and murmured words in English in a soothing voice. It felt better to have someone there with her, even if it was a stranger, and even if she had no idea what the woman was saying. Tuyet closed her eyes and tried to think of nothing.

After hours of drifting between troubled sleep and painful wakings, Tuyet was glad when night finally ended, and early morning light poured through the window. Now maybe Mom or Dad would come to take her home. She could hear carts wheeling up and down the hallway and the voices of men and women. But no one sounded familiar.

A woman, another stranger, entered the room carrying a tray of food. She set it down on a rolling table and propped Tuyet into a sitting position. All the while she chatted away to Tuyet in English.

Tuyet looked at the food on the tray. A glass of apple juice, a cup of green Jell-O, a bowl of brown broth. It didn't look like very much. A dull ache in the pit of her stomach reminded Tuyet that she was hungry, but she did not feel like eating. Her ankle wasn't the only thing screaming with pain. Now her knee, forced into an unnatural position by the cast, began to throb. She pushed the food away and closed her eyes. The woman said something in English, but Tuyet just hung her head.

Some time later, yet another uniformed woman came in. Tuyet was having trouble keeping track of them all. This one listened to Tuyet's heart and checked the fluid in the plastic bag on the pole. She frowned as she read notes from the clipboard she took from the end of Tuyet's bed.

She asked Tuyet a question in English. Tuyet shook her head. Couldn't they all just leave her alone?

In careful, slow English, Tuyet said, "I want Mom and Dad."

"Can't you see she's in pain?"

Tuyet's eyes flew open. Dad stood there, hands on hips, a shocked look on his face. A nurse hurried out the door.

He sounded angry with the hospital people. Maybe he and Mom hadn't realized what would be happening to her leg either. They had been told she'd be getting her ankle straightened, not a leg dipped in cement.

Mom sat on the edge of Tuyet's bed and leaned in, kissing her on the top of her head. Tuyet got a dusky floral whiff of Mom's favorite perfume. It smelled like—

"Home," pleaded Tuyet.

"Soon," said Mom, gently brushing a stray lock of hair behind Tuyet's ear.

The nurse came back, holding a hypodermic needle. Tuyet shook her head.

"For the pain," said Dad.

The nurse swabbed a spot on Tuyet's butt with a bit of cold, wet cotton. A small pinch, then warmth. Within seconds, Tuyet felt the pain ebbing away from her knee and ankle. She lay back against her pillow and sighed. It felt so wonderful to be free of the pain. How did Dad know she was hurting? She hadn't told him. How did he know what would help? It had never occurred to Tuyet to tell anyone about the pain. She'd never dreamed they'd be interested.

Mom held up the button that was attached to the cord. She pretended to push it, then pointed to the nurse, who was still holding the empty needle.

Now Tuyet understood! The button was for help. *All* kinds of help. Tuyet still wanted to go home, but she didn't feel quite so trapped now that she knew the nurses could make the pain go away. All she had to do was figure out a way to let them know what she needed.

Dad came to visit the following day. He examined her face carefully for signs of pain. Tuyet grinned at him. There was no pain. Dad's face broke out into a broad smile. He sat down on the bed and gave her a gentle hug. Tuyet clung to him, wishing she never had to let go.

After a few minutes, Dad unwrapped her arms from his neck and said something in English.

A young Vietnamese man stepped into the room and stood at the foot of her bed.

"Good day, Son Thi Anh Tuyet," he said in Vietnamese. "My name is Hoang Tuy. I am a student at this hospital."

Tuyet understood immediately that this man had come to help her. She thought back to how rude she had been when she first met Mrs. Nguyen. She wouldn't embarrass herself like that again. She sat up as straight as she could in her bed and bowed her head respectfully, in the traditional way.

Tuy returned Tuyet's greeting with a slight bow of his own. "Your father has asked me to explain what is happening to you."

"Thank you, Honorable Mr. Hoang," said Tuyet in Vietnamese.

"The cast on your leg," said Tuy, "has to stay on for six weeks."

"Honorable sir, will I need to stay in the hospital all that time?"

"No. You'll be here for a few more days and then you will go home."

"Mr. Hoang, why did they put this cement on my leg?" asked Tuyet. "I thought they were going to cut my ankle open."

"They did," said Tuy. "Your ankle has had surgery, and your foot is now straight. The cast is there to give your ankle some time to rest and heal."

"And in six weeks the cast comes off?"

Tuy nodded. "This week, the people at the hospital will show you how to walk with crutches. You'll be home before you know it."

"Thank you, Mr. Hoang," said Tuyet, bowing her head again. "It was kind of you to tell me this."

"If you would like, I could drop in later this week, to see how you are doing," said Tuy.

Tuyet smiled. "That would be kind of you, sir."

Tuy took one step toward the door, but Dad held up his hand. They spoke in English for a few minutes. Tuy left, but came back a few moments later with a pad of paper and a pen. He frowned in concentration as he wrote.

He tore off the top sheet and gave it to Tuyet. "Push your button when you need something," he said. "Once the nurse gets here, use this paper to point to the English words for what you need."

Tuyet looked at what he'd written. In one column were phrases in Vietnamese—*leg hurts, bathroom, hungry, thirsty, play*. Beside each Vietnamese phrase was a corresponding phrase in English.

Tuyet folded the paper carefully and held it to her chest. "Thank you, Mr. Hoang," she said, grinning. "This will help me very much."

Chapter Five
Home Again

The week went by slowly. Tuyet learned how to get around on crutches. The woman with the floral smock visited her every day, and she urged Tuyet to follow her to the playroom to be with the other children.

Tuyet preferred to stay in her room. Although she gathered up the courage to walk carefully down to the playroom, she stood by the doorway and watched the other children play, too shy to join in. None of them had almond eyes and golden skin like her. No one else had a leg in cement, or even crutches. It was hard to see why some of them needed to be in the hospital at all.

Mostly Tuyet played by herself or stared at the fish in the aquarium as she waited for the woman to usher her back to her room. No matter how kind the staff was or how interesting the toys were, Tuyet could not overcome her shyness. She longed to go home, to be with her family.

Sometimes at night, the nightmare would come back. It always seemed to be about the airplane, but other parts of it changed. In one dream, Tuyet was alone on the Hercules, searching frantically through boxes and storage areas, calling for Lara, Beth, Aaron, Mom, and Dad. Another time, she stood on the pavement in the sweltering heat and watched the airplane take off, her family pounding at the windows, trying to get out.

Dad came at visiting hour every day, but he never brought Aaron, Beth, or Lara with him. Children weren't allowed to visit. And most days Mom had to stay home to look after the children while Dad was at the hospital.

Finally, the day arrived.

Tuyet dressed in a pink striped shirt and a pair of wide bell-bottoms, which fit over her cast. She wore her one red shoe, and she stretched the red knit slipper over the foot of her cast. She wanted to walk out of the hospital on her own two legs and her crutches, but the staff insisted she leave in a wheelchair. Dad left a few minutes before she did because he had to get the car from the parking lot.

When the nurse pushed Tuyet's wheelchair into the elevator, Tuyet was surprised to see an adult with two good legs being pushed in a wheelchair as well. That made her feel better. They weren't making her take the wheelchair because of her leg; they made everyone leave that way.

Tuyet's heart filled with joy when the outside doors glided open and there was Dad, leaning against the car and smiling from ear to ear. Four ribbons were wrapped securely around his hand, and bobbing above his head, attached to the ribbons, were four big round balls—a red, a yellow, a pink, and a blue.

Dad gently lifted her from the wheelchair and

lowered her into the back so that her cast was lying across the seat. He tucked a pillow against the small of her back so she wasn't leaning directly on the door. Once she was settled, he sat down on the edge of the back seat and carefully unwound the ribbons from his hand.

"These are for you, Tuyet," he said, wrapping the ribbons around her hand.

She giggled as her father struggled to get the bobbing balls to stay inside the car. He shoved the last one in and closed the back door, then climbed into the driver's seat. He grinned and pointed to the balls. "*Balloons.*"

Tuyet watched the balloons tap gently against the roof of the car as they drove along the highway. It felt so good to be almost home.

When they pulled into the driveway, Beth ran outside to greet her, with Lara close behind. Mom followed with Aaron on her hip. The sight of her family together filled Tuyet with joy. This was all she'd ever wanted. A family of her own. A family to love.

Beth opened the back door of the car and Lara reached in, tugging on Tuyet's bell-bottoms. Tuyet slid gingerly forward until the foot of her cast touched the surface of the driveway. She carefully unwrapped the ribbons from around her hand. She separated out the yellow balloon and tied the ribbon around Lara's wrist. She gave the pink one to Beth and tied the red one to Aaron's arm. She kept the blue one for herself. It was exciting to have something to give her brother and sisters.

"Let me help you, sis," said Beth, her pink balloon pulling at her wrist. She wrapped both hands around one of Tuyet's.

But Tuyet shook her head. "Crutches?"

Dad got them from the trunk and steadied them in place so Tuyet could pull herself up to a standing position. Slowly, carefully, she walked across the driveway. It was more difficult to maneuver her cast on the driveway; it wasn't smooth like the hospital floors. The walkway was smoother than the driveway, but it was still hard work. Beth ran ahead of her and held open the door. Tuyet was proud of herself as she stepped through the front door.

But then she stopped. How would she manage to get up the six carpeted steps that led to the living room? She thought of how easy it had been to get up and down these steps before the surgery. In fact, she had never given these steps much thought before.

"I can carry you up to the top," said Dad, making a lifting motion with his arms.

Tuyet shook her head.

This was something Tuyet had to do on her own, but she did let Dad hold her blue balloon. She gingerly placed the rubber bottoms of her crutches on the lowest step and held them steady. She stepped onto the lowest stair with her good foot, then struggled to pull up her cement-encased leg to the same level. For one dizzy moment, she thought she was going to fall off, but Dad stood behind her, ready to catch her.

Tuyet looked up. Mom stood at the top, smiling encouragingly. Beth and Lara had scrambled up the stairs and were now sitting cross-legged on the shag carpeting on the living-room level, their balloons floating above their heads. Aaron sat cuddled between them.

"You can do it, sis!" said Beth.

Tuyet looked up at her siblings and smiled.

One step at a time.

Her face was covered with sweat by the time she got up to the living-room level. It took her a moment to catch her breath.

She surveyed the room, expecting it to look as it had before she'd gone to the hospital. But now the sofa had been made into a daybed, with a new pillow and blanket.

"For you," said Mom.

Leaning heavily on her crutches Tuyet managed to get over to the sofa, and then nearly fell into it. What a wonderful, cozy place! From her daybed, Tuyet could look out the front window. She could see through to the kitchen too. There was a television in the kitchen, and Mom had turned it toward the living room so that Tuyet could see it from her spot on the sofa. Tuyet was thrilled. She would be in the center of the family circle.

On that first night home, Tuyet had expected to sleep in her cozy spot on the floor between Beth and Lara's beds, but when she hobbled into her sisters' bedroom, she was shocked to see only the rug between the two beds.

Beth motioned for her to come and see the other room—the bedroom where she had spent her first night. Tuyet stepped in through the doorway of that other room. The bed was made up. The window was open a crack and a cool fresh breeze blew in through the curtains.

Tuyet pasted a smile on her face, but her heart ached with disappointment.

At the hospital, she'd had to sleep in a room all by herself and she'd hated it. All week, she had longed to be home, to be surrounded by her family. Why couldn't she sleep in her cozy nest on the floor between her sisters?

Tuyet tried hard to look happy as she played at the kitchen table with her sisters all afternoon, and she was thrilled when Mom cooked chicken and rice for dinner, and served sweet, fresh pineapple for dessert. It tasted so much better than the hospital food. But when bedtime loomed, try as she might, Tuyet couldn't keep the heaviness from her heart.

Once she and her siblings finished brushing their teeth, Tuyet stumped down the hall to Beth and Lara's room. Dad stood in the doorway while Tuyet pointed to the empty spot between their beds.

"Tuyet sleep?" she said.

Dad pointed to the cast on her leg. "You can't sleep on the floor anymore, my dear daughter," he said. "You could hurt yourself."

Tuyet's eyes filled with tears, but Dad just shook his head. Tuyet slowly made her way to her own bedroom.

Mom sat on the bed with Holly Hobbie on her lap. Tuyet changed into her pajamas and leaned her crutches up against the wall within easy reach of the bed. She slipped under the covers with her doll. Then Mom and Dad tucked her in and kissed her good night.

Mom turned off the main light in Tuyet's room, but it wasn't completely dark. Tuyet could see the shape of her dresser, the outline of the window, and the curtains fluttering gently. She thought of her sisters in the room next to her and longed to be with them.

Tuyet hugged her doll and tried to sleep. This bed seemed more comfortable than she remembered. In fact, it was a lot more comfortable than the hospital bed. She reached over with one hand and felt the cool wood of one crutch. She could go into her sisters' room anytime she wanted. But for now, she'd rest her eyes, in this soft and cozy bed.

Before she knew it, she was sound asleep.

In the morning, she woke up feeling happy and loved. Tuyet smiled to herself at the thought of it. Now that she had a family, she didn't have to worry about being in the exact same room with them all of the time. They were all the same family and they were a part of her. Tuyet was home.

5-1   *The Morris family home, circa 1975*

Chapter Six
Brady Bunch

As the days went by, Tuyet became adept at getting around on her crutches. Inside the cast, her leg itched like crazy. She longed to be able to scratch her ankle, but at least itchy skin was better than pain. Maybe the itching was a sign of healing.

Tuyet had counted out on the kitchen calendar the forty-two days that she'd have her cast on. June eighteenth was the day it was to come off.

The days settled into a routine. She played with Beth, Lara, and Aaron in the sandbox when the weather was nice. Beth and Lara would point to things and tell her the English names. Tuyet would repeat after them, "Shovel, pail, sandbox...swing." She tried to play on the swing too, but it took all her concentration just to sit on the seat and balance herself with her cement-encased foot planted firmly on the ground.

When she was too tired to sit outside, she would sit on the daybed and look out the front window at the older boys who lived next door. She longed to be able to run and kick and play as they did.

Mom liked to watch soap operas on the television when Aaron took his afternoon nap. Tuyet would color quietly or flip through books with Beth and Lara, who would point at pictures and tell her the English words.

After the soap operas were over, the sisters could choose what to watch. Tuyet had not paid much attention to the television before her surgery. She had preferred to play outside as much as possible. Now that she was forced to rest her leg, the stories on TV broke up the monotony of her day. Tuyet's favorite show was *The Brady Bunch*, and it was fun to figure out what the story was about. Each time an actor said a word that Tuyet recognized, she would repeat it: cat, cake, sneeze, doll. She loved that it was about a mom and a dad with a lot of kids, just like her family.

But on *The Brady Bunch*, all the children had white skin and round eyes.

After seeing the show for the first time, Tuyet hobbled into the bathroom and balanced herself against the sink in front of the mirror. She tried to pull her eyes into a round shape with her fingers.

Lara pounded on the bathroom door. "Let me in."

Tuyet did not answer.

Lara pushed the door open. Tuyet quickly took her fingers away from her face, but her sister saw what she had been doing.

Lara stepped up onto the bathroom stool so that the reflection of her face was level with Tuyet's. She touched the image of Tuyet's left eye.

"Brown," she said.

Tuyet grinned. She placed one of her own fingers on the reflection of Lara's right eye. "Brown," she said.

Tuyet gazed at herself and her sister in the mirror.

Of Mom and Dad's four children, only one was

white like on *The Brady Bunch*, and that was Beth. Mom and Dad said that Beth was "homemade."

Aaron had come from Vietnam just like Tuyet, and he'd been a Morris since he was a newborn baby.

Lara had also been a baby when she was adopted. She had been born in a place called Calcutta. Tuyet loved the warm richness of Lara's skin and the fact that her youngest sister's eyes were as deep and brown as her own and Aaron's, yet they were round like Beth's. They all looked different, but they were a family just the same.

Tuyet loved being a Morris.

Chapter Seven
Church

Usually on Sunday mornings, Mom went to church, and she took Beth, Lara, and Aaron with her. Before the surgery Tuyet had gone with them, but ever since her return from the hospital, she had been allowed to stay home with Dad, who was not a churchgoer. Tuyet looked forward to these times with her father. They would play, and later she would help him prepare Sunday brunch for the family.

But on the Sunday about a week before her cast was scheduled to come off, Mom told Tuyet to get dressed for church.

Tuyet looked from Mom to Dad in confusion. Why did she have to go to church and miss her special time with Dad? Didn't Mom realize how much Tuyet cherished Sunday mornings? And didn't Mom know how embarrassing it would be for Tuyet to have to maneuver across the church parking lot, up the steps, and down the aisle with her cast and crutches?

Mom put her hands on her hips. "Scoot, Tuyet," she said. "I don't want to be late."

Resigned, Tuyet hobbled to her bedroom. Mom had laid out a beautiful new pair of blue bell-bottomed pants, and a patterned pink and blue top. Tuyet wished she could wear a pretty dress like Beth's favorite red one, or Lara's shiny yellow one, but the new pants fit perfectly over her cast and wouldn't get in the way of her crutches. As she buttoned up her new blouse, she smiled to herself. She would miss spending the morning with Dad, but it was a treat to wear such beautiful clothes.

She sat on the bed and pulled the red knitted slipper over the foot of her cast, then slipped her right foot into her shiny red shoe.

Dad waved good-bye as Mom hoisted Aaron onto her hip. She guided her three daughters out the front door and into the car.

Beth and Lara settled in the front seat with Aaron nestled between them. Tuyet slid into the back, sitting sideways so her knee was straight. Mom put Tuyet's crutches into the trunk, and got into the driver's seat.

When they arrived at the church, Mom circled the parking lot to look for a spot, but all the nearest ones were taken. Mom pulled close to the church entrance and rolled down her window.

Tuyet saw a familiar woman at the bottom of the church steps.

"Pam!" called Mom.

The woman turned. She waved to Mom. Then her face broke into a huge grin when she saw Tuyet through the back window.

Tuyet waved back. She knew Mrs. MacDonald well. On the very first Sunday that Tuyet had gone to church, she had been embarrassed, so afraid that people would stare at her. But it had been a wonderful experience. And after the service, Mrs. MacDonald had given Tuyet a doll—her precious Holly Hobbie.

Mrs. MacDonald gathered Aaron into her arms and Mom took Tuyet's crutches from the trunk. She held them in place while Tuyet slid out the back door and pulled herself into a standing position. Beth and Lara scrambled out the front seat.

"Thank you, Pam," said Mom, getting back into the car.

Tuyet watched as Mom zoomed away to find a parking spot.

Tuyet took one step forward on her crutches and nearly lost her balance when the tip of her left crutch landed on a stone.

Mrs. MacDonald's eyes widened in alarm. "Let me carry you in," she said.

Tuyet shook her head.

Beth explained, "Tuyet likes to do things by herself."

Mrs. MacDonald kept pace with Tuyet, taking one slow step at a time along with her. By the time they got to the top step, Mom had joined them, breathless from hurrying. Mrs. MacDonald passed Aaron over to Mom, and she went on ahead with the other children to find a pew.

Tuyet could feel the sweat break out across her brow as she stepped in through the entryway of the church.

Was it her imagination, or had everyone turned to stare at her as she slowly made her way down the center aisle? With every step she took, Tuyet's face burned with embarrassment. She kept her eyes to the ground, placing her crutches carefully so she wouldn't trip.

When she was halfway up the aisle, Tuyet paused for a moment to see where her sisters were sitting. As she surveyed the congregation, she realized that people were not staring at her. Most had their heads bowed in prayer. The few who were turned toward her smiled in encouragement. Tuyet breathed in deeply and let it out again. It would all be okay.

When she finally got to the pew where Mom was settling Beth, Lara, and Aaron, Tuyet hesitated. The pew was too narrow for her to get into with her crutches—and even if she managed that, what about her cast? It came to just below her knee, so she could bend her leg to sit, but only for short periods, because after that, the weight of the cast made her knee ache.

Mom looked from Tuyet to the pew and saw the problem. She slipped out of her spot and found the minister. He brought out a small chair and sat it at the end of the pew. Tuyet sat down with relief, grateful to stretch her leg out in front of her, but she could almost feel the stares of the congregation at the back of her head. Again she wondered why Mom had made her come to church. Couldn't she have waited one more week?

But then the singing started. Tuyet closed her eyes and listened. She didn't know the words or these particular songs, but the strong voices rising up together filled her with joy. At the orphanage in Saigon, whenever the nuns sang or led the children in song, the sounds of war were drowned out and forgotten, if only for a few moments. Here, the songs were different, but the effect was the same. Tuyet felt safe and wrapped in love.

It was hard with her crutches, but Tuyet was glad that Mom had brought her here.

Chapter Eight
June 8, 1975

Much as Tuyet loved listening to the music, going to church in her cast had been an exhausting experience. By the time they returned home, Tuyet was grumpy. She wanted nothing more than to go inside, flop down on her daybed, and take a nap.

Mom parked the car in the driveway, and Beth and Lara ran inside giggling, not waiting for Tuyet or Mom and Aaron. Tuyet became even grumpier.

Mom held Aaron on her hip and opened the car door for Tuyet, and then she held the front door of the house as Tuyet limped in. Every bone in Tuyet's body ached.

But when she stepped into the living room, she saw

bright balloons bobbing on ribbons. She remembered the four balloons that Dad had brought to the hospital and she no longer felt tired. Balloons meant fun.

In the kitchen, Dad was holding a big plate with something that looked like a cake. But Tuyet's heart clutched with fear. The cake was on fire!

Mom and Dad and Lara and Beth all shouted together, "Surprise! Happy Birthday!"

They were grinning and giggling, but Tuyet was confused.

"Fire!" she said, pointing to the cake. "Bad."

Dad put the cake down on the kitchen table. The fire was coming from flaming sticks that had been pushed into the cake, and they continued to burn. Didn't Mom and Dad know how dangerous fire was? Someone had to put that fire out!

Tuyet hobbled to the sink, grabbed a glass from the draining tray, and filled it with water. She turned to the cake and was about to dump the water on it—when Mom grabbed the glass from her just in time.

"It's okay, Tuyet," she said soothingly.

Tuyet slumped down into a chair, mesmerized by the sight of the burning cake. This must be another strange Canadian custom—buying balloons and burning cakes.

"Blow out the candles," said Beth, dancing in one spot with the excitement of it all.

Tuyet shook her head, confused.

"I'll show you," said Beth. She leaned in until her face was just inches from the fire. Tuyet was frozen in fear for her sister. Why didn't Mom or Dad pull her away?

Beth took in a deep breath. Her lips formed a tiny O. Then she blew out, hard. One of the fire sticks stopped burning.

Beth pointed to Tuyet, and then she pointed to the cake.

Tuyet understood at last. It was her job to put out the fires. She stood up and filled her lungs with air. She blew with every bit of breath she had. The fire sticks went out. She slumped back down into her chair.

Beth grabbed Lara's hand and they both got up from the kitchen table and darted down the hallway.

They came back moments later, each holding a brightly colored box tied with ribbon.

Lara thrust hers into Tuyet's hands. "Open mine first."

Tuyet understood; the pretty box was a present. She held it in both hands and bowed her head. "Thank you."

"Open," said Lara.

Tuyet stared at her sister, mystified.

Lara took the present back. "Like this," she said and she ripped the colorful paper.

Tuyet gasped. Why was Lara ruining the pretty box? Would Dad and Mom get mad at her? But when Tuyet looked across the table, she saw that her parents were still smiling. This was surely the strangest Canadian custom of all, ripping up little boxes.

Lara thrust the half-opened present back into Tuyet's hands, and Tuyet pulled off the rest of the paper to reveal a plain box. She opened it. Inside were small hard candies in a rainbow of colors. Tuyet set the box down on the table.

Mom shook her head. "Present," she said, pointing at the box of candies. "For you," she added, resting a finger on Tuyet's chest. "All for you."

Tuyet was stunned. The box of candy was for her? But why?

Beth set her box in front of Tuyet. "Open it," she said, her voice trembling with excitement. "I hope you like it."

Tuyet ripped the patterned paper off the second box. Inside was a bright pink hairbrush along with a matching set of barrettes.

She grinned and turned to her sister. "Thank you, Beth."

Beth clapped her hands. "I am so happy that you like it."

Lara and Beth each brought over another box, and another. Tuyet opened them all. It hardly mattered what was inside, it was just so much fun, ripping the paper and opening the boxes. What made Tuyet happiest was seeing the joy on her parents' faces as she and her sisters and brother giggled.

When she was finished, Dad served brunch, and then Mom cut each of them a slice of cake.

That night in bed, Tuyet hugged Holly Hobbie tight and thought about the wonderful day she'd had:

the balloons, the colorful boxes, the fiery cake—Lara and Beth's excitement.

Tuyet still had no idea what a birthday was, but it had been the best day ever.

Chapter Nine
Can you walk, Tuyet?

When they pushed open the door to the Fracture Clinic at McMaster Hospital, Tuyet was astonished to see so many adults and children with casts—on their legs, feet, wrists, and arms. She and Dad found the only two empty chairs that were next to each other in the crowded room, so Tuyet sat in one of them and propped her crutches in front of the other to save it for Dad while he checked in at reception.

They waited for what seemed like hours, but Tuyet didn't mind. She watched the other people in the room and tried to imagine why they had cemented body parts. Maybe some of them had fallen and broken their bones. Maybe some had polio like she did. It was amazing that bones could be fixed this way, by putting them in cement for weeks and weeks.

A white-uniformed woman came into the waiting room and looked down at the clipboard she was holding. "Tuyet Morris?"

Dad held her crutches upright and Tuyet stood. They followed the nurse into a small room with a cot, a desk, a chair against the wall, and a stool on sliding castors. The nurse pointed to the cot and said to Tuyet, "That's for you."

Tuyet sat on the side of the cot and Dad helped her swing her legs up onto it, then he pulled off her red slipper. They were barely settled when a man came in holding a mean-looking instrument with a long electrical cord and sharp metal teeth.

He plugged in the instrument, sat down on the stool, and pulled up close to Tuyet's cot. He smiled and said, "This won't touch your skin. It's only to open the cast."

Tuyet didn't understand. She looked over at her father.

"It will be okay," he said gently.

The man flipped a switch on the instrument. It made a loud, grinding buzz.

Tuyet's heart pounded. Surely he wasn't going to use that electric saw to remove the cement? What if it cut all the way down to her leg? She gripped the sides of her cot.

He brought the saw to her leg.

Tuyet's father gave her a nod of encouragement, and she held her breath. She could feel her entire leg vibrating and the buzz became a high-pitched whirr.

Under her breath, she chanted, "Please don't cut my leg open, please don't cut my leg…"

She wanted to close her eyes, to make it all go away, but that was impossible. She was paralyzed by the sight of the whirring saw teeth making a clean, grooved line down the entire length of her cast. When he got to the bottom, he took a pair of snub-nosed clippers and snipped through the bottom edge of her cast. Then he rolled his stool in closer and carefully snipped the top edge of her cast.

He motioned for her to flip over and he repeated the same exercise on the back of her cast. Dad helped her get into a sitting position when the man had finished grinding. Tuyet watched the man spread open her cast with a thing that looked like salad tongs. Beneath the cast, her leg was wrapped in white cloth. The man snipped some more—then the cloth and cast were off her leg.

Tuyet looked down at her leg and gasped. Bits of white fluff and plaster still clung to her skin, but her leg was perfect and straight. Her foot wasn't curled under her ankle anymore and the calluses were gone. Tuyet put her two legs side by side. The left one was still about six inches shorter than the right, but it was straight. She wiggled her toes and grinned.

Out of Dad's pocket came the red slipper. Tuyet pulled it over her tiny perfect left foot.

Would she be able to walk on it like this? Tuyet didn't know.

Tuyet was used to the weight of her cast, so using the crutches without the cast made her feel out of balance.

They didn't go straight home after leaving the fracture clinic. Dad parked on the street in front of a corner store.

Why were they shopping now? Tuyet was anxious to get home so she could show Mom her perfect foot and her straight ankle.

There was quite a bit of traffic on the road, so Dad stood protectively by the passenger door while Tuyet got out. He held her steady as she hopped beside him to the trunk of the car to get her crutches.

They walked into the store together.

It was packed with all shapes and sizes of crutches, wheelchairs, canes, and scooters. Some of the crutches and canes hung from the ceiling on hooks and others hung from racks on the walls. The wheelchairs were collapsed and stacked against one of the walls, and the shelves and bins were filled with all sorts of parts, bolts, and fasteners. Tuyet had to maneuver carefully with her crutches so she wouldn't knock anything over.

Tuyet watched Dad walk up to a friendly-looking man with glasses poised on the tip of his nose. They exchanged a few words, and then the man walked over to where Tuyet stood.

"I'm Joe," he said. His eyes looked kind as he peered

at Tuyet over his glasses. Then he looked down at her foot. "Let's measure you for a brace."

He motioned her to balance on a platform and he measured the dimensions of her left leg. Then he measured the length of her right leg for comparison. He also measured both feet.

"Come back in two weeks," he said.

Tuyet was anxious to show off her perfect foot to her family, but it had been such an exhausting day. By the time they pulled into the driveway, her eyes were beginning to droop.

Dad offered to carry her inside, but Tuyet didn't want Mom to think there was something wrong. After all, this was her first day with a straight foot. Shouldn't she be able to get around better than when she had the cement on her leg?

It took less strength for her to hobble with her crutches now that the cast was gone, but she felt out of balance. By the time she got to the front door and up the stairs to the living room, her back was aching.

Mom, Lara, Beth, and Aaron crowded around, grinning with excitement.

"I want to see your new foot," said Beth.

Tuyet hopped over to the daybed and sank into it with a grateful sigh. Aaron toddled up to her and pulled at her red slipper. Tuyet smiled. Even Aaron was excited to see her perfect foot. She helped him tug the slipper off then held up her foot for everyone to see.

Lara clapped her hands. "It is beautiful," she said.

Mom sat down on the daybed and handed Tuyet a gift-wrapped box. It wasn't her birthday, but it was a special occasion. Tuyet tore off the paper with glee.

Inside was a single red shoe. It was exactly the same as the one she wore on her right foot, only smaller. Tuyet slipped her perfect new foot into the shoe.

She hugged Mom and admired her feet. She couldn't remember ever wearing a pair of shoes that matched.

Chapter Ten
Strength

While Tuyet waited for her brace to be made, Dad took her to a place called a physiotherapy clinic. It was something like a hospital, except that she didn't have to stay overnight or have her leg cut open. But like a hospital, the therapists were dressed in white and they looked after patients who had weak arms or legs.

One of the walls was covered from floor to ceiling with a mirror; the other walls had cheerful wallpaper with tiny flowers. A woman was soaking her arm in a swirling tub of water. A man sat in a chair while a physiotherapist guided one of his feet into a vat of hot liquid. The man pulled his foot out and Tuyet stared in amazement as it started to cool. His foot was completely enclosed in wax!

Tuyet wondered if her own foot would be plunged in swirling water or hot wax. She wouldn't mind that. It looked almost like fun. But a white-coated woman led her instead to a parallel set of railings that faced the mirror. Dad held onto her crutches and the woman motioned for Tuyet to hold onto one end and to walk toward the mirror.

As the woman chatted away to her, Tuyet wished more than ever that she could speak English. Couldn't the physiotherapist see that she wasn't able to walk without her crutches? How was she supposed to hold onto the railings and get to the end with only one foot on the ground? But the woman smiled and motioned for her to move forward.

Tuyet felt the coolness of the wood as she wrapped the fingers of her left hand around the left railing. Then she gripped the right railing with her other hand. Using the full strength of both her arms, she lifted her body up and hopped forward one step.

The woman motioned with her hands for Tuyet to keep moving.

"You can do it, my dear," said Dad.

Tuyet looked up at him. He smiled. That gave her strength. Tuyet looked at the reflection of her two legs. The one that did all the work, and the other one that hung uselessly. This woman had a reason for making her do this odd walk. Tuyet hopped again with a combination of arm strength and determination. And again. One step at a time, she got all the way to the mirror.

Thank goodness it was over. Sweat rolled into her eyes.

But the woman was not finished. She led Tuyet over to a chair and motioned for her to sit. Then she pulled up another chair and sat beside Tuyet. The woman planted her two feet on the floor in front of her. She placed something floppy covered with flowery cotton on one of her own ankles. Slowly, she raised her ankle until her knee was straight.

"Now, your turn," she said, giving the floppy thing to Tuyet and pointing to her left ankle.

Tuyet was surprised by how heavy the thing was. It seemed to be filled with sand. She placed the odd sandbag on her own small ankle. Frowning with effort, she slowly lifted the bag until her knee was straight. The physiotherapist made her do this exercise so many times that Tuyet's leg began to feel like rubber.

The woman handed the sandbag to Dad. "She needs to do this exercise at home each day."

The physiotherapist then lifted Tuyet onto a high table and had her lie flat on her back. She straightened Tuyet's leg, then put one hand on her kneecap and pushed down. She placed her other hand on the sole of Tuyet's foot and pushed firmly toward Tuyet's knee.

"Try to push your foot into my hand," said the woman.

From her hand motions, Tuyet realized what the woman wanted her to do, but it felt so uncomfortable. Even when Tuyet didn't push back, the pressure from the woman's hand pressing down on her knee was almost unbearable. But when Tuyet did push back, the pain was even worse.

But Tuyet tried not to think about all of that. Instead, she remembered what Mrs. Nguyen had told her. All these things they were doing to her leg were to help her to walk. Tuyet gulped in a lungful of air and then pushed hard with her foot.

"Good work," the physiotherapist said. "Now you are done for the day."

Each day Tuyet worked until she was exhausted. At the end of each session, all she wanted to do was go home, curl up on the sofa, and watch *The Brady Bunch*. But each day before she went home, a physiotherapist would bend and push her foot and ankle. Her weak leg would ache and tingle from the treatment, and Tuyet wished that she didn't have to do it, but she could feel her leg getting stronger. Tuyet began to dream of a time when she might walk without crutches.

After two weeks of physiotherapy, Dad took Tuyet back to Joe's store. He had a leg brace built just for her. The brace was made up of a parallel set of metal rods that started above Tuyet's knee and attached to a platform under her foot. The rods were straight above and below the knee, but right at the knee they each had a joint so they could bend with her. The whole device was held together with leather straps.

10-1   *An updated version of the leather and metal brace that Tuyet wore.*

Joe helped strap Tuyet into the leg brace. The bulk of it made her weak leg almost as wide as her good leg, but her foot did not touch the ground. Tuyet wondered how she was supposed to walk in this thing.

Joe held up one finger and said, "I'll be right back." Then he walked down the hallway and stepped into a room at the end. Moments later he came back, holding a shoebox. He set it in front of Tuyet and removed the lid.

Tuyet was shocked by what she saw. Inside the box was the ugliest pair of shoes she had ever seen. They were brown and looked like men's shoes. One was flat, and the other had a sole built up six inches.

Tuyet removed her beautiful red shoe from her good foot. She slipped on the ugly flat brown shoe, and Dad helped her lace it up. Next, she slipped off the small red shoe from her left foot. She slipped the built-up shoe over the brace and over the tiny foot. Dad helped her lace that one up too.

Tuyet looked down. The right shoe was so ugly compared to her beautiful red shoe, but it wasn't nearly as ugly as the huge built-up brown shoe that she had to wear on her left foot. Tuyet thought she would weep from the sheer ugliness of her footwear.

But she didn't.

Instead, Tuyet surprised herself by smiling.

"It fits well," said Joe. He unlaced the shoe and slipped it off, then unbuckled the brace.

Tuyet sat down and Dad slipped her red shoes back onto her feet. She frowned in confusion. Wasn't she going to be wearing the brace and the ugly shoes

10-2   *A pair of orthopedic shoes similar to Tuyet's*

from now on? But Dad pointed at what Joe was doing.

Joe removed the insert from the built-up shoe and squeezed gel inside. He fitted the base of the brace inside the shoe and put the insert back in, pressing down firmly so the gluey gel connected the shoe and the brace together.

"In one week, the gel will set and your brace will be ready," said Joe.

The week ticked by slowly. Much as Tuyet loved her shiny red shoes, she looked forward to having two feet on the ground. When they finally stepped into the store a week later, she was beside herself with excitement.

Joe greeted them with a smile. He brought out her brace with the shoe attached and, with careful precision, showed Tuyet how to put it on. What had been gel now felt solid under the insert. Once the brace was done up and both shoes laced, Joe got her to walk with her crutches and the brace from one end of the store to the other. He made some tiny adjustments, then asked her to walk again. Once more, he made an adjustment.

Finally, he was satisfied.

Tuyet bowed her head. "Thank you, Mr. Joe," she said carefully.

She grinned broadly as she and Dad walked out of the store together. Maybe the shoes were ugly, but they got the job done. For the first time in her memory, both feet were solidly on the ground at the same time.

Chapter Eleven
One Step At A Time

Tuyet used the crutches to get back to the car, and she unlocked the knee joints on the brace so she could sit. The leather and metal dug into her thigh, but she was determined to get used to the brace.

Tuyet looked out the window as Dad drove back to Brantford. They had been back and forth from Hamilton to Brantford so many times that the half-hour trip had become a routine. Dad would chat with her in English, and she would try to figure out what he was saying. Sometimes it was easy; she learned the words for colors and vehicles. But other times she had no idea what he was talking about. She smiled at him and nodded whether she could understand or not. Tuyet loved the sound of Dad's voice almost as much as she found comfort in his snores at night.

Tuyet's mind filled with thoughts about how much her life had changed in the past few months. She wondered what she'd be doing right now if she hadn't been rescued. Would she have stayed in the orphanage with the nuns—the only child left? Or would soldiers have found her? The last image she had of Saigon was a city filled with soldiers and tanks, and people running away in fear.

She looked out Dad's side window and saw the steep granite wall of Hamilton Mountain. She turned her head and looked out her own window. From where they were on the highway, she could see down the mountain and a vast area of houses. She wondered if any of the children who had been with her in the rescue from Saigon now lived in those houses. Tuyet thought of Linh, the older girl she had met on the airlift. Linh had visited her a few times and Tuyet had been ecstatic. She hoped they would see each other again, but Linh never came back. The disappearance of Linh was just one of many losses she had endured. Most of the time she tried not to think of bad things, but sometimes she couldn't help it.

Dad reached out and squeezed her hand. Tuyet's eyes filled with tears of gratitude. Even though they didn't speak the same language, Dad always understood what she was thinking.

Tuyet looked down at the way her braced left leg bulked out under her bell-bottoms. What a smart tool the brace was. To think that people could make a leg work, first by dipping it in cement, and then wrapping it up in leather and metal. She felt through her pant leg to find the metal joints at her knee, then with both hands she straightened her leg out slightly so it was more comfortable. It would take getting used to, wearing this brace, but she was determined to make it work.

Before she knew it, they were home.

Dad parked the car in the driveway and pulled Tuyet's crutches out of the trunk. He walked around to the passenger side, but he knew better than to try to help Tuyet out. Instead, he smiled, holding her crutches, and waited for her to get out on her own.

Tuyet swiveled in the seat so that both of her ugly brown shoes rested on the driveway. She pulled herself to a standing position by holding onto the car door, then pushed the knee hinges on the brace so that her left leg was straight and the hinges locked in place.

Tuyet held onto the crutches. The new sensation of wearing the brace made Tuyet feel out of balance, but she took a deep breath and stepped forward with the built-up shoe. So far so good.

With Dad by her side, Tuyet stepped slowly to the front door. It took strength and willpower and concentration, but Tuyet was determined to do it on her own. When she got through the front door to the inside steps, she was thankful that she had done all those physiotherapy exercises. Would she have been able to climb the steps on her own if she hadn't strengthened her leg? Probably not.

Tuyet kept the shoes and brace on. She wanted to practice walking around the house. She used the walls for balance and practiced maneuvering around toys and furniture.

When it was time to go to bed, Mom helped her take the brace off. Her skin had red rub marks where the straps had been buckled, and her leg felt tingly from the exertion.

"You are doing so well with your brace," said Mom as she gently massaged lotion into the sore spots on Tuyet's leg.

Tuyet felt heavy with exhaustion. She got into her pajamas and fell asleep quickly. Until—

She was jolted awake in the middle of the night. She sat up in bed and looked over at her ugly brown shoes, one with the brace sticking out of it. They sat neatly at the baseboard beside her crutches. She got out of bed and picked up the plain brown shoe that she wore on her right foot. With the help of her crutches, she carried the brown shoe out to the living room and down the six steps to the front entrance. She gazed at the row of her family's shoes in the moonlight. Six pairs were lined up—one pair for each family member. Tuyet's big and little red shoes sat between Beth and Lara's shoes. She took her red shoes out of the row and replaced them with the one brown shoe.

Tuyet leaned back on her crutches to admire the row of shoes. The red shoes were pretty, but they were only for show. The brown shoes would help her walk.

When she fell back to sleep, she dreamed of standing upright without holding onto crutches. She dreamed of walking on her own.

Chapter Twelve
The Hardest Things

The time before she came to Canada seemed like a distant nightmare as the days lengthened into summer and the sun warmed Tuyet's face. In July, Dad set up a wading pool in the backyard and filled it with icy water.

Tuyet loved playing in the pool on the hot summer days with Beth, Lara and Aaron. She didn't need her brace, and the cool water soothed her muscles and skin. Sometimes cousins would visit; other times, family friends would bring their children to splash and play with the Morris children. Tuyet loved playing, and she loved being surrounded by so many children.

But Tuyet especially loved holding Baby Aaron on her lap. She showed him the blades of grass and how to make them whistle, just as Dad had shown her on her first days in Brantford. She loved breathing in the scent of Aaron's downy hair and feeling the warmth of his chubby body as she wrapped her arms around him.

But holding Aaron made her heart ache with a loss that had no words. Wisps of memory would come back, of another boy, long ago. A boy who may have been her brother. She hugged Aaron tight and whispered in his ear, "I love you, dear brother. Don't ever leave me."

Once, when she, Beth, and Lara were building a giant castle in the sandbox, Tuyet heard an ominous sound from above. Through the clouds she saw the silhouette of an airplane. A stream of pale dust was falling from the belly of the aircraft.

"Run!" Tuyet screamed. She grabbed Beth's hand and pulled her up. Then she scrabbled over to Lara and Aaron. "Inside, inside!"

Tuyet crawled toward the kitchen door, pushing and pulling Beth and Lara and Aaron as she went. "Not safe!" she cried.

Mom opened the sliding door and stepped outside. "Inside!" cried Tuyet, pointing to the sky. "Not safe!"

Mom looked up to the sky and saw the silhouette of a crop duster. She pointed. "Is that what's not safe?" she asked Tuyet.

Tuyet nodded. Bad things came out of airplanes. Bombs, poison, fire.

Mom picked up Tuyet and hugged her fiercely. "You are safe, my dear daughter. The airplane is dropping seeds, not bombs."

Tuyet didn't understand the words, but she could tell that Mom was not frightened. As she melted into her mother's reassuring embrace, she closed her eyes and tried to block her fear.

Mrs. Nguyen explained to Tuyet that when September came, she would go to school. "You will learn English there," she said. "And there will be lots of children like you. Children who speak languages other than English."

"Will any of them be on crutches?" asked Tuyet.

"I don't know," said Mrs. Nguyen. "But not all hurts show on the outside."

Tuyet nodded. This she understood.

Tuyet continued to go to physiotherapy. At the clinic she would do exercises without her brace, then put the brace on and do some more. She would watch herself in the mirror as she carefully stepped forward, wearing her brace and built-up shoe, but without holding onto her crutches. At first she could barely take a single step forward, but with patience and practice she gradually improved.

The hardest thing was to walk outside without the crutches. Lawns were uneven, and so were driveways and sidewalks. But that was another skill for Tuyet to practice. She would walk without her crutches close to the wall of the house or the wooden back porch, so if she lost her balance, she'd have something to hold on to.

One day, at the end of the summer, Tuyet walked all the way down to the end of her driveway without crutches. Her back ached and her face was red from the exertion, but she did it. And it felt exhilarating.

12-1   *Tuyet ready for school, holding her Holly Hobbie doll.*

She stood in front of her house and surveyed the street. This was the first time she had stood here on her own—on her own two feet.

Just then, she heard running footsteps from next door followed by a *thump* and a *whoosh*. A soccer ball bounded along the neighbor's lawn and rolled until it stopped just in front of her.

Tuyet looked up and saw the boys who lived next door. The younger one began to run toward the ball, but Tuyet held up her hand.

She carefully lifted her right foot until all her weight had shifted to her new perfect foot and the built-up shoe.

Then, with her other foot, she kicked the ball firmly, right back to them.

HISTORICAL NOTE
About the Orphan Airlifts

During the course of the Vietnam War, many Vietnamese children were left orphaned. Missionary groups from all over the world came to South Vietnam and tried to help the orphans, but supplies were hard to come by and the conditions in the orphanages were awful. When South Vietnam was captured, the North Vietnamese victors wanted to close down the orphanages. Healthy South Vietnamese orphans would go to families and be brought up as loyal communists. But children with disabilities—like Tuyet—would be killed. The children of American fathers, who were considered the enemy, would also be killed.

*B-1   Colonel "Hank" Henry, Base Commander of Canadian
Forces Base Trenton, welcomes the crew
of Service Flight 515 on their return from
Hong Kong and Saigon*

In the spring of 1975, most American troops had already left South Vietnam. Saigon, the capital city of South Vietnam, was about to be overtaken by the North Vietnamese forces.

The missionaries were desperate to get out as many orphans as they could before the fall of Saigon. On

April 2, 1975, fifty-seven orphans were airlifted out of Saigon on a World Airways plane. On April 4th, the first official "Operation Babylift" evacuation was to take place, but the plane crashed just after takeoff. Many orphans and care workers died.

The rescue operation described in *Last Airlift* was the last to arrive in Canada, and there were fifty-seven babies and children on the flight. The children arrived in Toronto on April 13, 1975. The flight was sponsored by the Ontario government and, unlike most of the rescue flights before it, the children on this flight were not pre-adopted. John and Dorothy Morris did not know that Tuyet would become their daughter until the day before they met her. In addition to Tuyet, John and Dorothy were parents to Beth, their birth daughter, Aaron, from Vietnam, and Lara, from Bangladesh.

On April 14, 2006, thirty-four of the original fifty-seven orphans met in Oakville, Ontario, for a reunion. They exchanged stories and toured Surrey Place.

Since that time, they have become like one big extended family. They have not yet been able to connect with all of the orphans from their flight. If you know one of them, please contact:

marsha@calla.com

B-2

Master Corporal Dave Melanson, a 426 Squadron Loadmaster with the Canadian Air Force on the relief flight, with two of the children

About Polio

Polio is an abbreviation for poliomyelitis, a virus that can be spread through contaminated food and water. Children are more often infected than adults.

When a person first contracts polio, they may have no symptoms at all, or perhaps a mild fever. Most people recover without long-lasting damage, but one in a hundred will have permanent paralysis, because the virus affects the central nervous system and destroys the nerve cells that make muscles work.

If a child's leg is damaged by polio, it stops growing and stops building muscle. The undamaged leg keeps on growing. This means that by the time a child becomes an adult, one leg could be six or eight inches longer than the other. And the short leg and foot will be weak and thin.

Polio can also stop the muscles in the foot and ankle from developing. When this happens, the damaged foot may turn inward. This is what happened to Tuyet. While she was at the orphanage, Tuyet taught herself to walk by putting all her weight on her anklebone or the side of her heel.

When a person walks on the side of their foot, they do even more damage to their ankle. Their posture is no longer straight, which can cause other health problems as well as pain.

Surgery to straighten the ankle makes it possible for a shoe and brace to be fitted, and this corrects posture so it no longer hurts to walk and other health problems do not develop. Best of all, it means the person will be able to walk on the sole of their foot instead of their ankle.

Up until the 1950s, polio was the most feared disease in North America. Thousands of children and adults had their arms, legs, and respiration permanently damaged because of polio. In 1955, the Salk vaccine was introduced, and the widespread use of the vaccine curtailed the spread of this terrible disease in North America. In 1962, the Sabin oral vaccine was introduced. It wasn't until the mid-1970s that Canada had polio under control. The US was declared polio-free in 1979. Canada was certified polio-free in 1994.

While North America is polio-free, the world is not so fortunate. In countries suffering from poverty or war, polio can still run rampant. The World Health Organization and the Centers for Disease Control and Prevention consider the eradication of polio to be a top world health priority. These organizations, along with UNICEF and Rotary International, have been working for decades toward the eradication of polio worldwide. Over the years, Rotary International volunteers and fundraisers around the world have helped immunize more than two billion children against polio. Since that time, the incidence of polio has declined by 99%. As long as one person is still infected, however, we are all at risk for its spread.

Further Resources for Parents and Teachers

Internet

- http://www.vietnambabylift.org
- http://www.vietnampix.com
  (Warning: an excellent site, but some graphic images
  are included.)
- Would you like to help make the world polio-free?
  Contact your local Rotary Club.
  The Rotary Foundation of Canada:
  www.trfcanada.org
- **Rotary International**: www.rotary.org
- *Joint initiative with Rotary, UNICEF, WHO,
  and the CDC:*
  Polio Global Eradication Initiative:
  www.polioeradication.org

Books

- *The War Cradle: Operation Babylift—The Untold Story*, by Shirley Peck-Barnes, Vintage Pressworks, 2000
- *In the Clear*, by Anne Laurel Carter, Orca Book Publishers, 2001
- *Dear Canada: To Stand On My Own: The Polio Epidemic Diary of Noreen Robertson, Saskatoon, Saskatchewan, 1937*, by Barbara Haworth-Attard, Scholastic Canada, 2010
- *Small Steps: The Year I Got Polio* (Anniversary Edition), by Peg Kehret, Albert Whitman & Company, 2000

Film

- *Daughter from Danang*, a co-presentation of ITVS and NAATA with *American Experience*; WGBH Boston; producer, Gail Dolgin; directors, Gail Dolgin and Vicente Franco.

Author's Note

Son Thi Anh Tuyet is now an adult, and she lives in my hometown of Brantford, Ontario. Her married name is Tuyet Yurczyszyn. She and her husband Darren bought the house Tuyet grew up in, and they have two happy, healthy children named Luke and Bria.

As part of my research, I interviewed many people. Special thanks to Thi Mai Murphy, Trent Kilner, Thanh Campbell, and Kit Spencer. Cliff Zacharias recounted his vivid memories of that fateful flight and shared his photographs. Special thanks to Dr. Georgiana Stanciu, Curator of the National Air Force Museum of Canada, and also Assistant Curator Hailey Latour. Many thanks to RCAF 426 Squadron historian Robert Fleming.

I would like to thank Dr. William Vivianni, Tuyet's orthopedic surgeon, for sharing his insight; and Joe Cottone of C&DC Orthopaedic Services, who has known Tuyet since she was a child and has been providing her with shoes and braces for all these decades.

Tuyet's sisters, Beth and Lara, were generous and helpful with their time and memories. Thank you, Beth, for connecting me with McMaster Archivist Anne McKeage, who not only guided me through the photography archives of McMaster University Medical Centre, but also took me on a tour of where Tuyet had stayed while at the hospital. Anne also kindly read the manuscript of *One Step at a Time*.

Tuyet's mother, Dorothy Morris, was amazing. Her detailed recall of Tuyet's earliest days in Brantford helped me rebuild that time with accuracy. I have such admiration for Dorothy and her late husband John for their unconditional love and acceptance of not just one, but three war orphans.

In addition to the personal interviews, I read American Babylift memoirs and also watched news clips and documentaries. I pored over weeks' worth of microfilm copies of the *Brantford Expositor* and accessed The *Globe and Mail* online historical database. The *Toronto Star*'s "Pages of the Past" online database was especially helpful, as they ran a series of articles following the day-to-day progress of the last Canadian airlift, from the children's escape from Saigon until their placement with their adoptive families. Staff writer Jim Robinson's articles were particularly detailed.

The surgery described in this book was just one of six corrective procedures that Tuyet endured over the years. If she had not received these surgeries, she would never have been able to walk. Tuyet had her final set of surgeries just before starting high school. Her short leg was lengthened and her long leg was shortened.

Back in the 1970s, parents were not allowed to stay with their children in the hospital. And back then, there were no services in place for patients who did not speak English. If Tuyet were a child now, the experience would not have been so terrifying.

Tuyet's actual birthday was on August 6th, not June 8th. Her mother and father had misread her Vietnamese birth certificate, which had listed her birthday as 06/08/1967. So on August 6th, she received a second birthday cake.

Special thanks to Gail Winskill: I would not have written nonfiction without your encouragement.

Ann Featherstone: thank you again for helping me make the words shine.

When I initially approached Tuyet about this project, I was going to write it as a novel rather than non-fiction. Many of Tuyet's memories from that time were suppressed, so I was going to piece together a story of one orphan based on the experiences of many. But as I recreated these experiences from my research, an interesting thing happened. In small flashes, Tuyet began to remember more. I read every word of this story aloud to her and, as I did, she would stop and correct me. As time went on, her memories became clearer. Once, she called me the day after a marathon reading session; a random scene from television had just sparked a suppressed memory. When *Last Airlift* was complete, Tuyet was overwhelmed by the fact that it was, in fact, her own story that had been reclaimed.

Although Mrs. Nguyen and Hoang Tuy (Tuy is his first name) are real people, their names are inventions. Tuyet still has gaps in her childhood memories, but she will never forget the kindness of these two individuals. Linh, Tuyet's friend, is also real. Her name has been changed to protect her privacy. After she arrived in Canada and was adopted, it was determined that she was not an orphan at all, but the daughter of diplomats. She was reunited with her parents and moved to the United States. Tuyet never heard from her again.

Tuyet is my hero. The brave little girl whose early life was fraught with sadness and pain has grown into a remarkable woman filled with joy, generosity, and love.

Thank you, Tuyet, for sharing your story with the world.

B-3   *The author with Tuyet, spring 2011*

MARSHA FORCHUK SKRYPUCH managed to hide the fact that she couldn't read until grade four, when she failed the provincial reading exam. Too proud to ask for help, she taught herself how to read by taking out the fattest book she could find in the children's section of the Brantford Public Library, *The Adventures of Oliver Twist* by Charles Dickens. She had to renew the book for a whole year, but she not only managed to finish it, she learned to love books. Reading that big, fat novel, she says, was a turning point in her life.

Today, Marsha is the author of more than a dozen historical picture books, chapter books, and juvenile and young adult novels. She has received numerous awards and nominations for her work.

Her books include *The War Below* (In Canada, *Underground Soldier*), which has been nominated for the North Carolina Young Adult Book Award and the CYBILS Award; *Making Bombs for Hitler*, winner of the Iowa Teen Award, the Manitoba Young Readers' Choice Award, and the OLA Silver Birch Fiction Award, among other honors; and *Too Young to Esacpe: A Vietnamese Child Waits to be Reunited with her Family*, which is a USBBY Oustanding International Book, an ILA Notable Book for a Global Society, a Junior Library Guild selection, and an NCTA Freeman Book Award Honorable Mention.

In 2008, in recognition of her outstanding achievement in the development of the culture of Ukraine, Marsha was awarded the Order of Princess Olha, which was bestowed upon her personally by President Victor Yushchenko. Marsha lives in Brantford, Ontario.

TUYET would like to add her thanks.

Mom and Dad: Thank you so much for all the love. You have made me the way I am today. Also a BIG THANKS for saving my life!
To my dear husband, Darren: you are my rock.
And to my precious kids, Luke and Bria:
you fill my heart with joy.

15-1   *The Morris children in 1976. Front, from left, Beth, Aaron and Lara. Behind, Tuyet.*

Photo Credits

Last Airlift

1-1: Birth certificate–courtesy of Dorothy Morris; 1-2: helicopters–Getty Images/Archive Holdings Inc.; 2-1: tanks in Saigon–© Jacques Pavlovsky/Sygma/ CORBIS; 2-2: civilians flee–© Jacques Pavlovsky/ Sygma/CORBIS; 2-3: Hercules 130–courtesy of Major (Retired) Cliff Zacharias; 3-1: boxed babies–courtesy of 426 Squadron, 8 Wing/ Canadian Forces Base Trenton; 3-2: Major Cliff Zacharias–courtesy of Major (Retired) Cliff Zacharias; 4-1: aid workers assist children; 4-2: children on rescue flight; 4-3: aid workers in Hong

Kong–426 Squadron, 8 Wing/Canadian Forces Base Trenton; 4-4: Tuyet arriving in Canada; 5-1: orphan with care worker; 5-2: medical staff examines baby; 5-3: toddler with new bear–Doug Griffin/Toronto Star/GetStock; 6-1: Adoption Order form–courtesy of Dorothy Morris; 6-2: Morris Family; 7-1: newspaper headline–Brantford Expositor; 8-1: Tuyet's passport photos; 9-1: Tuyet's Vietnamese handwriting; 10-1: Tuyet with Linh, 1975; 10-2: Tuyet and siblings–courtesy of Dorothy Morris;

One Step at a Time

1-1: Morris Family–Brantford Expositor; 3-1: McMaster University Medical Centre–Public Affairs Photograph Collection, Hamilton Health Sciences. Archives of Hamilton Health Sciences and the Faculty of Health Sciences, McMaster University; 3-2: McMaster University Medical Centre operating room–Public Affairs Photograph Collection, Hamilton Health Sciences. Archives of Hamilton

Health Sciences and the Faculty of Health Sciences, McMaster University; 5-1: Morris Family home–courtesy of Dorothy Morris; 10-1: Knee and foot brace–Metal and Leather KAFO/photo courtesy of Becker Orthopedic; 10-2: Custom made shoes–courtesy of Raymond Strasburg, Pedorthist, FootwearConsultants. com, Paul M. Bass facility at UT Southwestern Medical Center, Dallas Texas; 12-1: Tuyet with doll–courtesy of Dorothy Morris.

Back Matter

B-1: Canadian Forces Base Trenton–courtesy of Major (Retired) Cliff Zacharias; B-2: Corporal with 2 orphans–courtesy of 426 Squadron, 8 Wing/Canadian Forces Base Trenton; B-3: Marsha and Tuyet–Brian Thompson; B-4: Morris children, 1976–courtesy of Dorothy Morris.

Index